THRACE

CE

Neapolis Dicaea Maronia
Oesyme Abdera Doriscus Aps
Thasos Aerus

Samothrace Sestos Lampsacus Priapus
Imbros Abydus
Elaeus Dardanus
t.Athos Hellespont Sigeum TROY- Scepsis
LAND IDA MTS.
Lemnos Tenedos Antandrus
Assus Adramyttium MYSIA
Methymna Maestus R.
LESBOS Pergamum
Antissa Caicus R.
Pyrrha Mytilene Elaea
Atarneus
Scyrus Cyme LYDIA
Psyra Phocaea Hermus R.
Magnesia
Erythrae Sardis
CHIOS Clazomenae
Chios Teos Cayster R.
Lebedos Colophon
Carystus Ephesus
Notonium Magnesia
Andros Andros Samos Maeander R.
Ceos Tenos Icaria Samos Priene
Myus CARIA
Syros Mykonos Miletus
Delos Patmos Iassus
Paros Naxos Leros Halicarnassus
Siphnus Naxos
Cos Cos
Sicinus Amorgus Astypalaea Cnidus
Melos Ios Syme
Thera Anaphe Telus DORIS
Ialysus

PERSIAN EMPIRE

[signature]

Chelsea.

25th July 08

Ancient Greece

www.pocketessentials.com

Other books in this series by the same author

The Crusades

I hope you enjoy
reading this
Marian 25.7.08

Ancient Greece

MIKE PAINE

POCKET ESSENTIALS

This edition published in 2008 by Pocket Essentials
P.O.Box 394, Harpenden, Herts, AL5 1XJ
www.pocketessentials.com

Series Editor: Nick Rennison
Index & Proofs: Richard Howard

A CIP catalogue record for this book is available from the British Library.

ISBN 978-1-904048-245-7

2 4 6 8 10 9 7 5 3 1

Typeset by Avocet Typeset, Chilton, Aylesbury, Bucks
Printed and bound in Great Britain by J H Haynes & Co Ltd, Sparkford, Somerset

Acknowledgements

Thanks are due particularly to my editor, Nick Rennison, and my publisher, Ion Mills, for their support, particularly during the latter stages of the writing of this book.

Contents

Introduction:
The Geography of Greece

Introduction: The Geography of Greece

Today the country of Greece consists of the mainly mountainous land that forms the end of the Balkan peninsula and the numerous islands that lie in the Aegean Sea to its east, the Ionian Sea to the west, and the Mediterranean Sea to the south. Roughly comparable in size to England its glories similarly lie in the past. Civilisation reached it first from the south, before radiating northwards – and thus the great cultures and civilisations that dominate its past follow roughly this same path north. It borders Albania, Bulgaria and Macedonia to the north – the latter representing part of the ancient Greek kingdom of Macedonia, an entity divided between Greece, Bulgaria and Serbia at the end of the Balkan Wars (1912–13). From Macedonian Greece, the Balkan peninsula narrows, heading southeast, until we come across many of the famous classical settlements, from Thebes to Athens. To the southwest, connected to the mainland by a thin strip of land called the Isthmus of Corinth (named after the city at its southern end) is the Peloponnese, with Arcadia at its centre and Sparta to the south. Beyond this are the many islands, over 2,000 of them, that make up nearly 20% of the country. The Ionian Islands to the west include Ithaca, famed in antiquity as the home of Odysseus. In the southern Aegean are the Cyclades, some thirty islands, among them Delos and Naxos, whose prehistory saw a culture characterised today by mysterious sculptures of elegant, folded-arm nudes. Beyond them, towards the Turkish coast, are the Dodecanese whose largest isle, Rhodes, was famed for one of the Seven Wonders of the Ancient World – the Colossus. Further north along the Turkish coast are Samos, Chios and Lesbos – the latter home to the most famous female poet of classical times, Sappho. At the very southern end of the Aegean lies the largest of the Greek islands, Crete, home to the first true Greek civilisation in the second millennium before the birth of Christ.

Ancient Greece, however, extended further than this. First to be colonised at some point in prehistory was the western coast of Turkey. During the eighth century BC, colonies were founded along the southern Turkish coast and the Levant, and also in Sicily. The seventh and sixth centuries saw the time of greatest expansion. The Black Sea was ringed by Greek settlements; towns sprung up scattered across the Southern Italian littoral. Southern France, Corsica, Egypt, Libya, even Southern Spain close to the Straits of Gibraltar saw settlement by the Greeks.

The history of Ancient Greece at it simplest breaks down into three periods. In the first period, the story is of the great and mysterious civilisations that preceded Classical Greek society, the Minoans and the Mycenaeans. After their collapse and the subsequent Dark Age that followed comes the second period in which Greece follows a path that eventually leads to it enjoying the status of the most important cultural, military and political force among the countries bordering the Mediterranean at that time. The third period is the story of the Hellenistic Age, a time of new empires frequently in conflict with each other until their eventual conquest by the expanding Roman Empire. The story of the Ancient Greeks does not quite end there. As servants of Rome, their influence upon their rulers, socially and culturally, was as strong as it was when they were independent. Rome may have won the final military victory but it may not have won the cultural war.

Minoan and Mycenaean Greece

1. Minoan and Mycenaean Greece

At ancient and beautiful Smyrna – now the busy Turkish port of Izmir – Homer, the greatest poet of the Ancient Greeks, was born. Or so the inhabitants of that city claimed. They were not unique in this: numerous old cities of Greece vied with one another to claim the author of the two greatest epics, the *Iliad* and the *Odyssey*, as one of their own. The only evidence for his life is in the poems themselves – a few small details in the *Iliad* and the preponderance in the poem of the Ionic dialect hints that his home was somewhere along what is now the west coast of Turkey, or on one of the nearby isles. So Smyrna's conviction that his birthplace was somewhere along its sheltered bay is no more unlikely than many other such claims. In truth we know nothing of his life. Even the famous portrayal of him as a blind man is nothing more than a literary convention.

The Greeks themselves were aware of this. By the Hellenistic period, Greek scholars at the Library of Alexandria were speculating that different authors lay behind the two epics. In the present day we go even further than this, qualifying our understanding of Homer's role as author. Close analysis of the poems has made it clear that their origins were oral. Certain stock phrases – the famous 'wine-dark' sea for instance – and constructions (e.g. the frequent and similar descriptions of the heroes preparing themselves for battle) indicate that both poems in some form or other were recited by bardic figures using these rhetorical props to aid in their long recitations. We will never know to what extent each poem is the work of one man – not that this detracts from their importance and achievement as among the greatest literary works of western civilisation.

The *Iliad* has been tentatively dated as having been written in the early part of the eighth century, the *Odyssey* is thought in turn to have first been written down some fifty years later. These greatest of Greek poems are also the earliest to survive, written in the new script adopted by the Greeks from the Phoenicians, a semitic script that was probably first encountered by Greek traders visiting the Phoenician cities and ports of the eastern Mediterranean.

The *Iliad* is a tale of a Greek army in Asia Minor, a brief episode in the legendary ten-year Trojan War. The war itself begins after Paris, son of the Trojan King Priam, elopes with the fabled beauty Helen (Marlowe's 'face that launched a thousand ships, and burnt the topless towers of Ilium' in his Doctor Faustus), wife of Menelaus, King of Sparta. Under the command of Menelaus's brother,

Agamemnon, King of Mycenae, the Greek forces sail to Troy to recover Helen and punish the Trojans. They lay siege to the city for ten long years. Eventually, through the ruse of a great wooden horse whose hollow belly contains Greek soldiers (the source of the proverb 'Beware Greeks bearing gifts'), they enter and sack Troy. The *Iliad* is concerned with a brief episode of this war – the conflict between the impetuous and fiery Greek hero, Achilles, and the noble Trojan prince, Hector, and the events leading up to this mortal battle. It remains as vivid and exciting to read today as it did more than twenty-five centuries ago. Homer's battle-weary and battle-hardened veterans are as convincingly drawn as any soldiers in a modern war story – their suffering, their scheming, their bravery and the desperate and futile courage with which they lay down their lives remains as moving in an age of nuclear weapons as it did when the latest cutting-edge military technology was the chariot.

The *Iliad* is also the earliest Greek poem we know of that attempts to bring the myths of the Greeks to life. The role of myth in Greek culture is a complex one. In later centuries myths were viewed as entertaining stories of doubtful truth or subject matter for literature that enabled the writer to examine the human condition. In Homer's time it is likely that the myth of the Trojan War was regarded as a historical fact. Ironically enough, it was a similar conviction in the truth of that story that drove a young German businessman in the nineteenth century, Heinrich Schliemann, to attempt to discover the reality behind the myths. Schliemann, a prodigious linguist, was obsessed by the tale of Troy from childhood. After making his fortune, he retired at the age of 36 with the intention of devoting the rest of his life to uncovering the foundation of Homer's world. At Hisarlik, in northwest Turkey, he conducted digs at a mound there in the 1870s. Very quickly the discoveries he made –

gold jewelry, major fortifications – convinced him that he had found Homeric Troy. In fact he had found more than Homer's city – the town he uncovered went back much further in time. To Schliemann these discoveries meant that Homer had been vindicated. In later years he would return to attempt to enlarge upon this discovery. For the time being what he had found at Hisarlik contented the amateur archaeologist. Another part of the *Iliad* now drew his attention. Homer had made the leader of the Greeks King of Mycenae – why? In Classical times the town was nothing more than ruins. Ancient Greek writers subsequent to Homer – unimpressed by these ruins – had relocated Agamemnon's capital to other more impressive and thriving settlements such as Argos. With Homer in mind, and with the detail of Agamemnon's grave at Mycenae confirmed (at least in Schliemann's eyes) in the writings of Pausanias, a Greek of the second century AD, whose Description of Greece has long remained an invaluable guide for tourists, Schliemann began digging there in 1876. His touch had not deserted him. Graves were soon uncovered that contained fabulous treasures. One piece, a gold mask, left Schliemann convinced that he was staring at the very face of Agamemnon himself. The news swept through the Europe of the day, making the German a celebrity. Schliemann had made a major find: the first real evidence for the great Greek civilisation that held sway before the Dark Ages. The more romantic and extraordinary description of gazing into the long-dead features of a figure out of antiquity proved irresistible to Schliemann and the journalists of the late Victorian world, however.

Discoveries like these made by Schliemann and subsequent archaeologists have confirmed that a memory of the Bronze Age does lie hidden in parts of the *Iliad*, despite the impossibility of linking the tale with some real incident. Certain cities that thrived during that period and yet were abandoned by Homer's time figure more prominently than one might expect. Excavation has supported their predominance in the tale. Certain features of the warriors' gear – the great shields, the famous boar's tusk helmets – were no longer in use in the post-Dark Age period and clearly point to the recollection of some aspects of antiquity.

Schliemann's legacy has been hotly disputed. On the one hand he has been accurately described as the father of bronze age archaeology in the Mediterranean: on the other hand his detractors have gone so far as to claim that the treasure 'found' at Troy had actually been bought in local markets and then planted in the ground there by Schliemann himself. Excavations continue at Hisarlik to this day – the recent discovery of a new set of outer walls some distance from what was previously thought to be the perimeter of the citadel are bringing about a re-evaluation of the site. More surprises undoubtedly lie below the surface, waiting to be unearthed. The site appears to have been occupied for thousands of years – Homer's city was built on the ruins of other cities, and suffered the same fate itself. No proof has been found that confirms Homer's tale and yet such is its spell that arguments still persist as to which ruin most closely fits Priam's devastated capital. Without archaeological evidence, however, of a major Mycenaean presence in the vicinity, the *Iliad* will remain strictly fiction.

Schliemann came close to making a third major discovery. He had long wanted to excavate at a particular site on Crete, again inspired by the *Iliad*, but had been unable to come to a financial agreement with the owner of that piece of land. After his death, the British archaeologist Sir Arthur Evans was to make the breakthrough there at the turn of the century. Evans uncovered the huge palace of Knossos. The labyrinthine nature of the building he uncovered reminded Evans immediately of the legend of King Minos and his labyrinth. Evans called the new culture Minoan as a consequence – he had uncovered the first great Aegean civilisation.

Minoan civilisation first rose to prominence in the early part of the second millennium BC, a period marked by the construction of palaces and increased trade with the Aegean islands (particularly the Cyclades) and the Greek mainland to the north, and with Ancient Egypt and the Levant to the south. They utilised a form of writing that we now call Linear A – using it for a language that has yet to be identified. This thriving culture was temporarily interrupted by a series of earthquakes. Afterwards, new palaces were built, more impressive than their predecessors. They were decorated by beautiful frescoes showing youths leaping over bulls in mysterious rituals, rural scenes with wild animals and streams, depictions of women picking saffron in the fields. Primarily through the vehicle of its pottery, the influence of Cretan art became widespread in the eastern Mediterranean Sea.

The story of the end of Minoan civilisation is disputed. The massive eruption of the volcanic island of Thera brought devastation to the surrounding islands, including Crete (an event that has often been argued as the origin behind the story of the destruction of Atlantis, the legendary island that is first mentioned in the writings of Plato). A tsunami destroyed settlements on the north Cretan coast. Volcanic ash fell. The exquisite frescoes at Akrotiri on Thera were preserved under several feet of it until they were redis-covered in the twentieth century. The same ash would have ruined crops at the time. Yet the Cretans apparently recovered from this catastrophe. Later the island appears to have been ruled by Mycenaeans from the main-land. A new script, Linear B, came into use. Arthur Evans discovered many clay tablets at Knossos, covered in this script. His convic-tion that it was a form of Ancient Greek was never proven in his lifetime. It was to be

Michael Ventris, an architect by trade, who was to finally decipher Linear B in the 1950s, proving Evans' intuition to be correct. The language was indeed a form of Greek. These tablets had survived the three thousand years before Evans' excavation because they had been baked hard by the fires that seem to have marked the final destruction of Cretan society around the second half of the thirteenth century BC. An influx of invaders from Europe or Western Asia may have been ultimately responsible. Egyptian records of the time describe the chaos brought by unnamed Sea Peoples to the north who raided the various coasts of the eastern Mediterranean. Whether this represented a migration into the eastern Mediterranean by a number of new peoples or whether it was the result of a more war-like behaviour on the part of some of those already living there (or, in fact, was down to a combination of the two) remains unresolved. The great Athenian historian Thucydides speaks of the invasion of the

Dorians, the last legendary wave of Greek invaders to arrive in Greece, taking place at around this time. (The Greeks of the Classical Age regarded themselves as the descendants of both native inhabitants and/or foreign invaders.)

Uncertainties abound about both dates and developments. The excavations of Sir Flinders Petrie in various sites in Egypt yielded a range of Greek pottery. The dating therefore of Greek sites has proceeded from the scheme arrived at for Egyptian history. Much confusion remains. Even the relatively well-documented history of Egypt has been questioned (most recently by David Rohl). The written records that exist and have been translated from Linear B are generally no more than tallies of goods. In the absence of contemporary written documents, historians have fallen back on Egyptian and Hittite sources of the period, and these are by no means clear in their description of events in Greece. What the prime causes were behind the fall of both the Mycenaeans and the Minoans is unclear. Who the mysterious Sea Peoples were is likewise unknown. Future excavations may shed light on what happened. As it is the confident picture enjoyed by previous generations of this early period of Greek history has been deconstructed by modern rigorous analysis.

The Dark Age that followed the collapse of Mycenaean civilisation is, unsurprisingly, also a time of uncertainty and confusion. The traditional picture has been of a society reduced to destitution, a period when even the scripts of the Mycenaeans and Minoans were lost. The shining light of what is commonly seen as the pinnacle of Ancient Greek civilisation, fifth century Athens, is thus interpreted as the result of a long climb back from out of the abyss. What is problematic with this attitude is that not enough is known of the Dark Age and of the civilisations before it to be able to state exactly what was lost, and, on the other hand, what in later Greek culture is original to that culture. Recent discoveries have tended to confirm that a number of features that were thought to have their origins in the late Dark Age actually date back earlier than that (the synoecism of Athens for example). How much is owed to the Mycenaeans and Minoans by the later Greeks will never be entirely clear.

We do know that some definite changes occurred. One example is provided by the pottery of the period. Minoan and Mycenaean pottery was generally figurative – humans and animals were frequently the subject matter. The decorative elements were usually simple and in a free and spontaneous style. With the Dark Ages a new style arose, which we refer to as Geometric. Increasingly intricate patterns such as meanders appear, while the figurative element fades in importance, sometimes vanishing completely. Another such change is the virtual abandonment of some of the older centres of population – Mycenae, for instance, became a shadow of its former self. There was possibly a fall in population generally and there appears to have been a movement away from the coastal cities. This might have been due to frequent raids from the sea's direction. Trade with the outside world fell drastically. While we cannot necessarily ascertain when certain cultural developments occurred, we can, from the written sources that began to appear, describe the society and culture that was coming into place.

The end of the Dark Ages is traditionally marked by the date of the earliest recorded Olympian Games in 776 BC. The new period that begins at this point and continues until the decisive victory obtained by the Greeks against the Persians in 479 BC is referred to as Archaic Greece.

Archaic Greece

2. Archaic Greece

Religion, Myth and Ceremony

While the names of some of the Gods of the Ancient Greeks appear in Linear B texts from the Mycenaean period (Poseidon and Athena for example) the earliest and most important literary text mentioning them comes from the first major Greek poet to follow Homer, Hesiod, who lived in Boeotia in central Greece in the eighth century. Hesiod's poem the Theogony tells of 'how the first gods and earth came to be, and rivers, and the boundless sea with its raging swell, and the gleaming stars, and the wide heavens above, and the gods who were born of them'. In this great genealogy the generations of the gods are listed; those who rule currently from the top of Mount Olympus in Greece, their ancestors, and the various supernatural beings that came into being alongside them.

The ruler of the Gods was Zeus, whose parentage stretched back through his father, Cronos, to the very first created divinities. Zeus rose to supremacy despite his own father's attempts to devour him as an infant, and in the great battle against the giants – the Gigantomachy – he led the gods associated with him to victory. To his brother Poseidon he gave the rule of the Kingdom of the Sea; to his brother Hades he gave control of the Kingdom of the Dead. The world that was left beside these was his. With Zeus as king of the gods, among the notables at his court were his jealous wife Hera, goddess of childbirth and patron of the cities of Argos and Samos; his daughter Athena, goddess of war and wisdom, patron of Athens, who sprung into the world directly from Zeus's forehead; Aphrodite, goddess of love, worshipped notably at Corinth and on Cyprus, thought to have been born from the sea from the white foam produced from Zeus's grandfather's severed genitals when they were hurled there by Zeus's father; Hermes, messenger of the gods and chiefly associated with Arcadia where he was born; Dionysus, god of wine and nature, in whose honour were held Dionysia, festivals where his female followers were supposed to indulge in ecstatic and supernatural abandon; and Apollo, associated with the sun, whose numerous oracles throughout the Greek world (most notably on the mainland at Delphi) were famed for their pronouncements. Beside these were numerous others although most of the court fell into two groups: the children of Cronos – Zeus and his brothers and sisters – and the children of Zeus himself.

The roles of the gods were both fluid and numerous. Although Aphrodite was commonly seen as a goddess of love she could be associated instead with war – as was the case at towns such as Sparta and Thebes. To

the people of each town and city-state particular gods were held dear depending on asso-
ciations of birth or acts of involvement in the
history of that settlement. Particular places as
well as activities came under the purview of a
particular god – for instance Zeus was associated with both the home and hospitality.

In addition to the Gods a vast and incred-
ible population of supernatural beings filled
the cosmos. Some provided the role of opponents for the Gods such as the Titans who,
while once gods themselves, were to spend
eternity languishing beneath Tartarus (a part
of the underworld) as the punishment for
daring to wage war – the Titanomachia – on
Zeus and his followers. Others more
commonly provided the role of opponents
for heroes and demi-gods who were generally
the offspring of unions between gods and
humans. Amongst these were the Minotaur,
half-man half-bull, who Theseus was to slay in
the labyrinth; Medusa, the snake-haired and
winged Gorgon whose gaze turned flesh to

stone, who was to be beheaded by Perseus; Cerberus, the three-headed canine guardian of the gates of hell, who Heracles – the ancient world's strongest man – cowed and dragged up to the world's surface.

Many others filled a part-role in a story or a niche in creation: the winged horse, Pegasus, steed of Perseus; the three Fates, Clotho, Lachesis and Atropos, old women whose spinning determined the lives of all humans; the centaurs, half-man half-horse, the most famous of whom was Achilles' teacher, Chiron; the Cyclops, one-eyed and brutal giants, who were thought responsible by the Greeks for the great ruined Mycenaean settlements such as Mycenae or Tiryns.

The world was a most fantastic place, filled with such creatures. The story of Homer's *Odyssey*, the tale of its hero, Odysseus, and the ten-year journey he underwent attempting to return home after the end of the Trojan War, is littered with such creatures – the Cyclops;

the enchantress, Circe; the Sirens whose song lures sailors to their deaths; Scylla, the six-headed creature who reaches down from her cave to pluck out and then feast upon unwary sailors.

These fabulous gods and monsters were only part of the story. Much of Greek myth is concerned with the tales of Greek heroes. These stories had a function somewhere between history and entertainment. The story of mankind up until the end of the age of heroes was told in a great collection of poems by various authors called the Epic Cycle. Part of this cycle was concerned with the Trojan War. From the earliest of these, the Cypria, detailing the origins of the war, a sequence of poems followed that told the whole story through to the final return of the heroes and their eventual fates: *Iliad*, Aethiopis, Little *Iliad*, Iliu Persis, Nostoi, *Odyssey* and Telegonia. With the exception of the *Iliad* and the *Odyssey* nothing remains of this part of the cycle (although part of the

Telegonia may have come down to us in the form of the final books of the *Odyssey*).

Beside the Trojan saga other story cycles made up the Epic Cycle. Although these epics have not survived, many of the same stories appeared and reappeared (with occasional variations of detail) in the poems of other Ancient Greek writers. One such poem lost from the Epic Cycle was the Thebais, concerned with the early history of Thebes from its founding by Cadmus through the rule of Oedipus to the unsuccessful siege of the city by seven heroes. Our knowledge of Oedipus, the tragic figure who despite rescuing the city from the Sphinx by answering its riddle is doomed to unknowingly slay his father and marry his mother, comes to us from the great trilogy of plays by the fifth century Athenian dramatist, Sophocles, Oedipus the King, Oedipus at Colonus, and Antigone. The story of the siege survives in such works as the Seven Against Thebes by Sophocles' predecessor, Aeschylus.

Another great sequence of stories recounts

the life and exploits of the great, Theban strong man of Greek myth, Heracles (more commonly known by his latinized name, Hercules). The traditional Twelve Labours of Heracles feature among the collection of myths and tales called the Library of Apollodorus of Athens. (Despite its ancient attribution, the one thing we can say of its author was that he wasn't Apollodorus of Athens, a scholar of the second century BC, but was in fact an anonymous Greek writer living some two or three hundred years later.) One sequence of stories inevitably leads into another: in one of the Pythian odes by the fifth century lyric poet, Pindar, we hear of Heracles' time as part of the crew of the Argo. In the canonical tale of Jason's journey to Colchis in search of the Golden Fleece, the Argonautica of Apollonius of Rhodes (a third century scholar at the most famous library of the ancient world, the Library of Alexandria), Heracles' role as crewmate is confirmed. It is important to stress that ancient authors were not averse to changing the details of a story. In Homer's *Odyssey* Agamemnon rules from Mycenae; in Aeschylus's Agamemnon it is the town of Argos. In a third version the poet Simonides apparently located him in Sparta. Sometimes the motivation for these changes was political; at other times the reason will probably forever remain unknown.

Like the Gods, heroes were often inextricably linked to a particular city-state through birth or circumstance. Athens' great hero was Theseus who, for his city's sake, travelled to Crete to defeat the Minotaur. Later, becoming king of Athens, the legend states that he united the various communities of Attica under Athens.

These beliefs, and the expression of their faith in ritual, were an essential part of being Greek. Greek religion was very much a public thing. In group worship, whether secretive or open, an animal sacrifice offered up to the gods was the central act. Individuals might offer up a bloodless sacrifice of food or incense when engaged in personal prayer, or offer up wine, poured on the ground as an act of honouring gods or heroes or the dead (a libation) in a private setting, or as a ceremony as part of a meal or a festival.

Animal sacrifice could be used as a method of receiving guidance from the gods in the form of omens by examining the entrails of the sacrificial victim.

Most of these ceremonies were public – a few were more private affairs, such as the rituals of the cult of Demeter and Kore that took place at Eleusis, refered to as 'mysteries'. The nature of these events and what they meant to those taking part have been hotly debated in recent years.

Each settlement would have its own sacred sites or shrines. In addition to these there were more important sites of worship called sanctuaries that were recognised as holy throughout the Hellenic world. The four greatest of these were at Delphi, Isthmia, Nemea and Olympia (dedicated in order to

Apollo, Poseidon, Zeus, and then again Zeus). Festivals held at these places, generally every year, would attract Greeks from all parts of the Ancient World. Each of these was a celebration of a shared Greek culture. The most important was the Olympian Games, ancestor of our own Olympic Games, which took place every four years at Olympia. Crowns of wild olive were the prizes for the winners of chariot races, wrestling matches, boxing, the pentathlon, the stadion (a 200 metre race on foot) and pankration (a violent and dangerous form of unarmed combat utilising boxing, wrestling, kicking and strangling) among others. The Isthmian, Nemean and Pythian (the festival associated with Delphi) Games were similar events although later, in addition, musical competitions were added.

Festivals in general were an important part of Greek life. Apart from sport and religion, the arts in general were honoured under the guise of honouring the Muses. The Muses were goddesses whose specific concerns were the arts. Traditionally there were nine, each responsible for a particular endeavour: Calliope (epic poetry), Clio (history), Erato (lyric poetry), Euterpe (the flute), Melpomene (tragedy), Polyhymnia (hymns), Terpsichore (dance), Thalia (comedy), and Urania (astronomy). Poets competed against each other for prizes, as did dramatists. Festivals celebrated historical events; festivals marked the seasons. It is thought that Athens spent at least two months a year engaged in such festivities.

Politics and Identity

The Archaic period was a time of resurgence for the Greeks. Trade and economic expansion powered this revival. Trade routes were opened up throughout the Mediterranean and into the Black Sea. Each major city-state established colonies throughout those areas. Sometimes the impetus was political disagreement at home, sometimes the pressure of population growth contributed. Generally, however, trade was the determinant factor. The goods imported into Greece were not only material. Contact with the Phoenicians had provided a script, in Egypt (notably at the colony of Naukratis) the exposure to Egyptian art and culture was to prove tremendously influential on the development of Greek art (particularly sculpture) and culture. In Sicily and Southern Italy, the Greek colonies provided an opportunity for the cultural influences to flow the other way, hellenising the Etruscan and nascent Roman societies there. This increasing engagement with the world outside Greece is reflected in the subject matter of the *Odyssey*.

The most characteristic political feature was the polis or city-state. Physically, each was an area of land defined by either neighbouring poleis or geographical features – such as the sea – with a city at its heart. Politically it was a community of citizens. Each was a sovereign territory. In some cases the city-state was formed around an already existing city, in others, for example Mantinea or Sparta, a city was formed from existing smaller communities. The incorporation of these disparate groups into a larger whole is referred to as synoecism. Each polis had its own laws yet many of the political structures were common to all – groups of elders functioning as magistrates, for example. While the Mycenaean world had been ruled by kings (wanax), the city-states of Archaic Greece became essentially oligarchies (where power was exercised by a small group of the wealthy). For brief periods kingship returned in many poleis in the form of tyrants who were generally members of the aristocracy who enjoyed popular support – tyranny had none of the modern negative connotations at that time. However popular a tyrant may have been (the sixth century rule of Athens by Pisistratus – later followed by his sons Hippias and Hipparchus – was considered exemplary by many, including the Athenian historian Thucydides) the general trend was towards oligarchy.

Just as the political roles of kings were occupied by elected members of the aristocracy, so too were the religious roles parcelled out. In Athens in the sixth century the roles of the king were split between three archons or rulers, each elected annually. One had responsibility for general affairs of the city-state; another, the polemarchos, was in charge of military affairs; the third, the basileus (the original Greek term for king), occupied the religious role.

A different system existed in Sparta. Two kings ruled, aided by five magistrates called ephors who, like the archons, spent a year in office, and a council of elders, the gerousia. Other Dorian city-states also elected ephors.

The Ancient Greek sense of identity was multilayered. A farmer from a small village or demes in Attica, the territory of the city-state of Athens, would have considered himself

Athenian. Beyond this he was a Greek, part of a larger group of people who shared a common tongue and common geographic origins (the colonies set up throughout the Mediterranean remained tied to their cities of origin, even if they eventually won political independence). But in addition to these identities he was also an Ionian. This was a group marked by a particular dialect, and found in specific places. Part of the western coast of Asia Minor was called Ionia, and the ancestors of the inhabitants there were supposed to have emigrated from the Greek mainland in response to the invasion by the Greeks from the north, the Dorians. Thus certain city-states on the mainland saw themselves as Ionian, while others, such as Sparta, saw themselves as descended from the Dorian invaders. Other such groups existed. For example, the Achaeans were another group who have both been argued as invaders who came with the Dorians and conversely as an indigenous people, like the Ionians, who may have been the descendents of the Mycenaeans. And the Aeolians came from Boeotia and Thessaly originally and later colonised part of the coast of Asia Minor, naming it Aeolis. To further complicate matters, each group was split into tribes – Spartans were Dorians but could further describe themselves as either Hylleis, Dymanes or Pamphyloi – and these tribes were possibly found in each city-state that claim kinship to the larger groups.

These perceived differences were to support dissent on the greater political stage. Ionian poleis tended to side with other Ionian poleis: Dorians stuck together with their fellow Dorians. Athens used its non-Dorian background to claim autochthony – that its people were the true 'original' inhabitants as compared to Dorian latecomers like Sparta – and thus to claim a primacy among Greeks. This variety within Greek identity was a double-edged sword. It made for a vigorous culture but at times a disunited one.

The development of the city-states and the competition between them saw different candidates emerge as dominant forces over time. Corinth surged ahead early on, benefiting from its geographical location (close to both the Ionian and Aegean Seas, with a rich and fertile land). Argos, supposedly the oldest Dorian city, was the first to have its own coinage, and was the leading force in the Peloponnese until the rise of Sparta in the sixth century. Thebes enjoyed pre-eminence in central Greece, which it consolidated with its later control of the Boeotian League, an association of Boeotian cities and towns. Eventually, irresistibly, two city-states were to be recognised as leaders among the Greeks in the period that followed the Archaic age – Athens and Sparta. This was the Classical Age (479–338 BC), the zenith of Greek culture and society. The emergence of Greece as the most powerful force in the ancient Mediterranean is marked by the first conflict that united it – the Persian Wars.

Classical Greece

3. Classical Greece

The Persian Wars

While in the west, Greece continued with its quiet cultural revolution, in the east, empires were being forged. The Assyrians had enjoyed dominance over much of the Middle East for centuries. Now, to their east, two small kingdoms, Media and Persian Anshan, began to expand. Assyria's conquest of Egypt in 671 BC was its last major intervention in the affairs of the Ancient World. In 612 BC it was to fall before the Medes and a resurgent Babylon. Babylon smoothly passed over to the Persians in 539 BC. The Median Empire had already fallen to the Persians some ten years before that. One great Persian king, Cyrus, had been behind these recent acquisitions, eager to build an empire. In the process he swallowed up Lydia.

The Lydians generally enjoyed good relations with their neighbours to the west, the Greeks of Ionia. Lydia influenced the Greeks in many ways – their invention of metallic coinage soon spread to the west, for example. A common culture lay between both peoples. The reign of their last king, Croesus (who was proverbially wealthy), saw many Greek visitors to his court from both Ionia and the mainland. By the time of the fall of Babylon, Lydia was already in Persian hands. Sparta sent word to the Persians warning them that it would not remain uninvolved should Cyrus make a move on the Greek cities of Ionia. It was a hollow warning. Soon Ionia was also under Persian rule.

Cyrus's death led to his son Cambyses's succession in 529 BC. Cambyses carried on much as his father had done – he had conquered Egypt by 525 BC. The Persian Empire was arguably now the largest empire the world had ever seen. In another four years however Cambyses himself had died in uncertain circumstances and the throne had passed to a relative, Darius. Darius was as ambitious as his two predecessors. Persia was now on a collision course with Greece.

First, Darius attempted to deal with the Scythians to his north in central Asia. The route he chose took him across the Bosphorus, through Thrace and the eastern borders of Macedonia. Thrace was claimed as Persian; Macedonia, a little off the beaten track for the Persians, retained its independence, humbling itself before the might and glory of the great Emperor. The kingdom of Macedonia stood at the entrance to Greece. Its rulers claimed descent from the Greeks although the Greeks viewed them as occupying a position somewhere between backward cousins and barbarians. The Macedonians had no desire to become a province of Persia. They played a cunning diplomatic game from this point onwards, acquiescing to Persian demands in the hope of retaining their independence, while to their neighbours to the south they represented their actions as designed to prevent any further incursions into Greece by the mighty Persian army.

Sparta's complaints and threats regarding Ionia had already been brushed aside. Now the Persians befriended and gave support to the recently ousted Athenian tyrant Hippias, who arrived in Persian territory in 505 BC. The newly democratic Athenians were no more amused at this support for their enemy than the Spartans were at being belittled earlier.

The crunch came when conspiring in Ionia set off a rebellion there against the Persians. Individual cities attempted to cast off the Persian yoke. The degree of disorganisation and spontaneity of these revolts hampered an easy Persian response. It was not entirely obvious to Darius who was involved. The first city to declare independence was Miletos, whose appeal to Athens and Sparta for aid saw the dispatch of 15 triremes (warships) from Athens and a further 5 ships from Eretria in Euboea. As Darius subdued one rebellion in one city another would break out elsewhere. The revolt was put down finally in 494 BC after six years of sporadic conflict. Darius, still angry at the involvement of Athens and Eretria, sent envoys to numerous Greek city-states insisting upon their submission to Persia. Many agreed to his demands. The twin leaders of the Greek world, Athens and Sparta, were made of stubborner stuff. They expressed their refusal by executing the envoys he had sent to them. Darius had had enough. His first attempts to deal with this opposition collapsed when the first fleet he sent in response was destroyed by a storm in 492 BC. Two more years passed and then finally the Persian plan to subdue the Greeks took shape as an army of 25,000 Persians landed unopposed at the Bay of Marathon. The first Greco-Persian War was underway.

Darius was expecting little resistance.

Athens had had warning of what was coming. On the way there the Persians had attacked Naxos and burnt its capital. In return for the Eretrian support to the Ionian rebels Eretria was then sacked and much of its population captured and deported. The Athenians knew they couldn't face such a force alone. The Spartans, renowned for their military prowess, heard of the Persian army when a runner turned up, requesting aid for Athens. The Spartans, in the middle of a religious festival, claimed that they could not begin a war until the festival ended. The Persians were not about to wait. Athens, with a few men from its neighbour, Plataea, managed to put together an army of around 10,000 men who set off for the plain of Marathon.

The Persians were rumoured to have the ex-tyrant Hippias with them. Their hesitation over attacking the Athenians has been argued as due to a supposed coup that Hippias's supporters may have been about to launch in Athens in the Athenian army's absence. Whatever the reason, this delay was to be their downfall. The ten Athenian generals on arrival were unsure of what to do in the face of their opponent's superior numbers. Among them was an aristocrat by the name of Miltiades who had both served Darius in his campaign against the Scythians and afterwards been involved with the Ionian revolutionaries in their failed struggle for freedom. Through these experiences, Miltiades knew that the absence of the Persian cavalry represented Athens' best chance and, convincing the Athenian polemarchos, Callimachus, of the same, was instrumental in launching the attack.

Miltiades was proved right. In a decisive engagement, the Persian force was beaten by the numerically inferior Greeks. The Greek army was spread along a wide front with their weakest part being in the centre of their line. Here the Persians broke through and the two now separate halves of the Greek army rushed in to envelop them. Soon the battle was over. Persian ships hurriedly made their way to rescue the remnants of the fleeing Persian army, the victorious Greeks in pursuit. Legend has it that the Greeks lost 192 men: the Persians over 6,000. The story goes that an Athenian messenger ran the 25 miles back to Athens, announced the victory, and then died of exhaustion – this being the origin of the marathon as a race.

When the Spartans appeared it was all over bar the shouting. The Athenians had won a tremendous victory on behalf of Greece, and strengthened their claim to be the leaders of the Greek world. The Greeks were left alone for the remaining five years of Darius's rule. Upon his death his son Xerxes took the crown. At first, he was occupied putting down revolts among the Babylonians and Egyptians. Soon, however, his attention turned to the Greeks, nearly ten years after his father's defeat. Xerxes did not aim to make the same mistake in underestimating them.

In the period between the end of the first Greco-Persian War and the start of the second, due to the conviction of one man, the Athenians had not been idle. That man was Themistocles, who had risen to prominence in public life as archon three years before Marathon. Through his foresight, cunning and determination, he was to become the man who saved Greece from the Persians in the second war.

The period after the victory at Marathon was one in which the increasingly democratic Athenian people flexed their political muscles. The most infamous example was in the practise of ostracism. Named after the fragments of pottery on which the voters inscribed the name of their nominee – ostraka – ostracism was ostensibly a method whereby the people could choose to exile without trial someone who they thought presented a danger to the state. This law had been first introduced in 508 BC by Cleisthenes, an archon and supporter of democracy. It is a measure of how extreme an act it was held to be that it was not until 487 BC that the first ostracism took place. Four more followed before the Athenian public came to their senses and issued a general amnesty in 481 BC. The arguments for ostracising an individual had become so debased that by the fifth ostracism, that of Aristides 'the Just', a local yokel is famously reported to have declared that he voted for Aristides's exile merely because he was tired of hearing him endlessly referred to as 'the Just'.

Through this political minefield stepped Themistocles. The lesson of Persian numbers was not lost on him. He realised that the best defence against a huge Persian force would be by hampering their ability to support that force in Greece – the Greeks therefore needed a strong navy. His was a lonely voice. It was only, in the end, the combination of a disagreement between Athens and the nearby Greek island of Aegina (a conflict that Themistocles has been accused by some of agitating for as an excuse to build his navy) and the discovery of a new vein of silver in the Athenian mines at Laurium that brought about the construction of a huge Athenian fleet of 200 triremes. He also managed to convince the Spartans. By the time the Persians did invade the Spartans were able to contribute another 150 ships to the cause. The combined navy of 350 ships was possibly only a third of the size of the Persian fleet but without them the second war would have been lost.

War finally came in 480 BC. Xerxes army was huge – somewhere in the region of 150,000 men. His navy shadowed this force as it made its way overland towards Athens. Half the Greek city-states chickened out, and made their peace with the Persian leader. The size and slowness of the force gave the Greeks who had decided to resist time to prepare.

Under Themistocles the naval force sailed to meet the Persian ships at Artemisium. The Spartan king, Leonidas, led a force of around 7,000 men to hold off the Persian army at the narrow pass of Thermopylae (the 'hot gates' – a name derived from the hot sulphurous springs found there). For three days Leonidas kept the huge Persian force at bay. The next night, a contingent of Persian 'Immortals' (Xerxes's own fighting elite), aided by the Greek traitor Ephialtes, found a way through another pass to attack the Greeks from the rear. Leonidas managed to get the main body of the Greek force away in time but he himself elected to stay with a force of 300 Spartans, their helots (Spartan serfs occupying a place half-way between citizens and slaves), and somewhere in the region of 1,000 Boeotians to buy the Greeks some time with their lives. And die they all did, although many more Persians were killed in the battle to take the pass.

The story of the 300 Spartans and their

stand against impossible odds became one of the great tales of military heroics. Herodotus writes that 'knowing that their own death was coming to them from the men who had circled the mountain, (they) put forth their very utmost strength against the barbarians; they fought in a frenzy, with no regard to their lives.' Their bodies were buried where they fell. An inscription above the mound that contained the Spartan dead read:

Go tell the Spartans, stranger passing by,
That here obedient to their words we lie.

The cost to Xerxes in men was substantial and embittered the Persian leader. He had his men search through the corpses on the battle-field until they found the body of Leonidas, and finding him, had his head cut off and mounted on a pole. The Greeks had lost but the Spartan example in noble defeat was to spur them on.

The Greek fleet retreated from their battle

with the Persian force once news of the defeat at Thermopylae reached them. More damage had been done by a tremendous storm striking the Persian ships while the Greeks were moored in port than was achieved by the triremes in the subsequent confrontation between the two. None the less the Persian fleet vastly out-numbered the Greeks.

Meanwhile, the Persian army carried onward towards Athens to the south. The Greek fleet, one step ahead, had evacuated most of Athens by the time the Persians got there. The Persians left the Acropolis, the ancient civic heart of Athens, burning.

Before the war had commenced, the Greeks had sent a deputation to the sanctuary at Delphi, hoping to receive a good omen from the oracle there. The first response to their request for advice had horrified them. It began 'wretched ones, why sit you here? Flee and begone to remotest ends of earth'. Desperate they petitioned for a second opinion – and this time received a slightly less bleak foretelling that the Greeks would lose a battle at Salamis, an island next to the Athenian port of Piraeus. Themistocles argued that the oracle could and should be interpreted as describing the Persians losing a battle there. He convinced the Greeks to station their ships in the narrow Strait of Salamis. The Persian navy was tricked, its greater number of vessels lured into the too-narrow waterway after Themistocles sent a Greek to Xerxes during the night to convince him that the Greeks were intent on flight. Within the strait the Greek ships wreaked havoc. Xerxes sat on his throne on the mainland, expecting to watch the final destruction of the Greek navy. The dramatist Aeschylus, present at the battle on board a Greek ship, described the scene that met the Emperor's eyes in his play The Persians:

The Grecian warships, calculating, dashed Round, and encircled us; ships showed their belly:

No longer could we see the water, charged
With ships' wrecks and men's blood.
Corpses glutted beaches and the rocks.

Xerxes ordered the remains of his once-
proud fleet to retire, and returned with them
to Persia. His land army persisted, under the
command of one Mardonios. He tried to split
the Greeks by attempting to make peace with
the Athenians in return for restoring them
Athens. The Athenians refused. The final
battles took place in 479 BC. On land the
largest Greek army yet (around 35,000 men)
faced and decisively beat the Persians and
their Theban allies outside the town of
Plataea. Off the Asian coast at Mycale, a final
indignity was heaped on the Persians. Rather
than face the Athenian ships they beached
their own vessels and joined their army on
land in its fight against a Spartan force. They
lost.

Greece had successfully defeated, not once
but twice, one of the largest empires in the

world. In light of its defeats, Persia followed a different strategy. From now on it would concentrate on fostering division and dissension among the Greeks. Athens, too, agitated where it could. Athens supported a rebellion in Egypt around the middle of the fifth century. Eventually a confrontation between a large Athenian fleet of over 200 ships with the forces of Xerxes's successor, Artaxerxes I, led to the destruction of this Athenian fleet in 454 BC. A peace treaty was negotiated in 449 BC that was to last until the next great war involving the Greeks – this time, between Athens and Sparta.

The Classical World: Athens

The end of the war with Persia in 479 BC marked the start of a golden age for Athens. So keen were they to look forward that at least one of the heroes of the past was quickly forgotten. Themistocles was honoured in Sparta for his efforts in the war but received little recognition in Athens. Then Sparta objected to the Athenian plan for rebuilding its defensive walls (destroyed by the Persians) and Themistocles' active promotion of the rebuilding lost him friends in Sparta. Less than a decade after the end of the war, Themistocles found himself ostracised by the Athenians. He moved briefly to Argos, then in response to accusations of conspiracy with Persia made by the Spartans he set off again, eventually ending up in Asia Minor – governing a province for Artaxerxes I. The Athenians passed a sentence of death on him in his absence and he was to spend the rest of his life in the east.

The new leading figure in Athenian politics was the son of Miltiades, Cimon. The year after the end of the war a new organisation was formed: the Delian League. The purpose of this organisation was originally to provide a defensive union in case of Persian aggression. It became clear immediately that Athens intended using it however to pursue an active campaign in Ionia against the enemy. Sparta, however, was experiencing problems at home and, keen to avoid involvement overseas, declined to join. The history of the league is the story of increasing Athenian imperialism. Early on the league's support facilitated successful action against the Persians. In the 460s a fleet led by Cimon liberated cities in southern Anatolia. By this point, two incidents that illustrated Athenian intentions had occurred: Carystus was forced to join the league and Naxos, wishing to leave, was subjected to military action by way of response. Originally the league's treasury had been located on Delos – hence the name – but in 454 BC it was transferred to Athens. Ten years later the league of the 'Athenians and their allies' was commonly referred to as 'the cities the Athenians rule'. League funds were soon being used to pay for the restoration of those parts of Athens damaged by the Persians, and then to part-finance the war against Sparta.

Ironically, as Athens grew ever more impe-
rialist, internally it became ever more democratic. Political power gradually moved from
the aristocracy to the people. The Areopagus,
a council of ex-archons, diminished in importance. The command of the army and navy
moved from the sole polemarchos to the ten
elected generals (strategoi). The seeds of
reform were first sown by the early sixth
century politician Solon with his prohibitions
on enslavement for debt, his redistributions
of land and his political reorganisations.
Cleisthenes later that century introduced
reforms that facilitated greater democracy by
the introduction of the demoi as the unit of
political organisation in Athens. Each demes
was a local group of adult men and each
demes was represented on the major council
of 500 (the boule) that had much of the
responsibility for the running of the state.
While it was still the aristocracy who
provided the candidates for the important
political positions, more and more influence

was wielded by the common people. Democracy in Athens was not so much an expression of the equality of its inhabitants but more a recognition of the rights of political involvement by all. This 'all' did not truly encompass all of the population, needless to say. Women, slaves, foreigners and minors had no representation. Athenian men reached adulthood when they joined their father's deme at the age of 18. It is wise to keep in mind that the citizenry often constituted no more than 10% of the population of Athens.

On the Pnyx, a hill in Athens, around forty times a year, the main assembly of the people (the ekklesia) would meet in their thousands to vote on issues of foreign and domestic policy, or to call for political trials. Votes were determined by a rough show of hands. This assembly, although unable to make law, was able to elect the magistrates whose job law-making was. Any citizen over 20 could speak at this gathering. Full political participation did not come until the age of 30 whereupon the citizens were eligible to serve on juries, stand for election to the magistracy or to the boule. Would-be jurors gathered early in the morning in the Athenian Agora (an assembly/market-place) where they were picked by lot to serve.

With the absence of political parties, the crowds tended to follow the most effective or charismatic speakers. Thus effective public policy was often concentrated in the hands of a particularly gifted individual.

It is important to stress that Athenian democracy is merely the most well-known brand of Greece democracy – it was neither the only nor even the first. Nor was the trend towards democracy a constant: city-states swung to and fro. In fact there were so many varieties of organisation that there were nearly as many political systems as there were city-states. It is also worth considering the other great difference between contemporary democratic representation and Athenian democracy: six thousand could be present at the ekklesia, expressing their will.

After the Battle of Plataea the Athenians had decided to leave the ruined Acropolis as a memorial. The 'Peace of Callias' made between the Persians and the Athenians in 449 BC, the continued wealth that poured out of the Laurium silver mines (not forgetting the deep pockets of the Delian League) and a new political leadership led to the decision to embark upon an ambitious plan of public building.

The new leader was the man more closely identified with the golden age of Athens than any other – Pericles. Cimon's fall from grace was confirmed by his ostracism in 461 BC. Increased tension between Sparta and Athens had made Cimon's panhellenic views too pro-Spartan for the public's taste. Pericles was an aristocrat, related to Cleisthenes on his mother's side, but more importantly he was a democrat and a nationalist. He was an impressive speaker, a clever politician, and a man on a mission to make Athens truly great.

Some impressive public building had been started before Cimon's fall. The famous Long Walls – two parallel defensive walls four miles long that connected Athens to Piraeus, its port – were in the process of being constructed. Pericles' aim was to improve upon the public grandeur of Athens that had been established under the reign of the tyrant Pisistratus in the middle of the sixth century. Part of the legacy of this period of construction is the most famous Greek building of all – the Parthenon. The money poured into these projects, and the general sense that only the best was good enough for Athenians, led to a tremendous flourishing of the arts in this period.

Art, Literature and Thought in Classical Greece

The most visible contribution the arts made to classical Athens was in the field of architecture. Most of the evolution of Greek architectural styles occurred in the seventh and sixth centuries. What would have impressed visitors to Athens in the classical period was the material. Much of the construction elsewhere in Greece utilised limestone; the quarries at Pentelicon enabled the Athenians to use marble. The temple of Athena Parthenos (Athena the Virgin) otherwise known as the Parthenon was famed for more than its material, however. Its architects, Callicrates and Ictinus, perfected the Doric form of architecture with this building. The sculptures and frieze – the latter celebrating the dead of Marathon – were of the highest quality. This commitment to excellence and the ability to pay for it attracted the finest craftsmen.

Inside the Parthenon the visitor would have been awed by the sight of one of the most famous pieces of Greek sculpture. Phidias's portrayal of Athena was 40 feet high, wooden and covered with ivory, jewels, paint, and over a ton of gold. For this, and his similarly huge statue of Zeus at Olympia, Phidias was accounted the greatest of all ancient sculptors. It was an art form in which the Greeks generally excelled. From its crude origins in the Dark Age, public sculpture was always important to the Greeks. The Archaic period saw the influence of Egyptian sculpture dominate in the more naturalistic portrayals of kouroi and korai (representations of male and female youths respectively). The classical period marks the perfection of Greek sculpture. The fidelity to life shown by Phidias of Athens and his contemporary Polyclitus of Argos influenced the following generations. Sculptors travelled across the Greek world, fulfilling commissions from cities keen to display their good taste and importance.

While Greek sculpture has survived – although often in the form of Hellenistic or Roman copies – little Greek painting has. Painters were celebrated and much written about whether they worked on frescos or wooden panels, painting portraits or landscapes. Statues were painted – the plainness of those that occupy contemporary museums give little indication of the vibrant or even gaudy colours that once covered their surfaces.

The one form of painting that has survived variously is vase painting. As with sculpture, the tradition of vase painting goes back beyond recorded memory. The measure of the respect held for these decorators was that by the late Archaic, the name of the painter often accompanied the name of the potter. The images are commonly taken from myth, the names of the gods and men pictured written above or beside them on the vase. Two techniques predominated in the Archaic and Classical periods. The first, invented in Corinth in the eighth century, was black-figure painting; the second, invented in Athens in the late sixth century was red-figure painting. The effects of the latter depended upon brushwork; the former on engraving. Athens established a name for itself and its decorated vases were exported in large numbers to the rest of the Greek world. In Southern Italy in particular, Athenian vase painters were to prove influential on the development of the art there.

Since the origins of Greek literature in the works of Homer, many new forms had developed. Greek prose was a late developer. Its earliest appearances are in the form of laws. After Homer and Hesiod, the epic was now challenged by the rise of the lyric or the elegiac poem. Alcaeus and Sappho, both writing on the isle of Lesbos in the sixth century, were famed for their Ionian lyric verse. Simonides was praised for his command of the elegy. Alcman of Sparta and Stesichorus of Sicily were renowned for their use of the choral lyric, a form with a Dorian tradition.

The great poet of the lyric form was Pindar, a Boeotian, born around 518 BC. Fame struck Pindar as a youth: he had received a commission from Thessaly by the age of 20. He was known throughout the

Mediterranean, from Sicily to Asia Minor, from Greece to North Africa. It is likely that he travelled to most of these places in response to the demands of patrons. Much of his writing was in the form of choral victory odes that marked the performances of winning athletes at festivals and many of these poems were publicly performed at ceremonies to celebrate these victories.

In one particular form of poetry Athens excelled: the verse drama. Three writers of tragedy and one of comedy from fifth century Athens stand head and shoulders above any others of the Ancient World. Tragedy came first, a development from the dithyramb, a choral song in honour of Dionysus, and the satyr play. The first great Athenian figure, Aeschylus (525–456 BC), expanded the form from one actor and a chorus to two actors with the chorus occupying a reduced role. Only 7 of his 90 plays survive complete. His most famous work is the Oresteia trilogy, a bleak retelling of the murder of Agamemnon by his wife and her lover, and how this act is revenged by his children. Sophocles (496–406 BC), in his turn, introduced a third actor allowing for a greater complexity, as is notable in his Theban Plays, a trilogy retelling the grim tale of Oedipus who murdered his father and married his mother. The third and last of this tragic triumvirate was Euripides (484–406 BC), who introduces a greater strain of realism into his characterisations, one absent in the work of the other two writers. Euripides' work also betrays the scepticism of his time when belief in the gods and in the stories of old had to a large extent dissipated.

Aristophanes (450–388 BC) is the only writer of what is termed 'Old Comedy' whose work has come down to us. In Aristophanes' plays nothing is sacrosanct. Other writers, politicians are all subject to his merciless wit and extraordinarily funny abuse.

The occasion for their performance would

have been at the Dionysia, the festival of
Dionysus held in Athens at the end of March.
Three tragedians each presented a satyr play
and three tragedies in competition with each
other. Five comedies, each with a different
author competed for a separate prize.

Prose in Classical Athens won lasting
renown in two forms: history and philosophy.

The most famous philosopher of antiquity
was Socrates (469–399 BC). Many Greek
philosophers preceded him. The earliest we
know of was one Thales of Miletus who
claimed that everything came originally from
the water, a view he supported by his finds of
fossil sea animals far inland. Anaximenes of
Miletus claimed it was air rather than water
that gave birth to the world. Heraclitus was
the first to talk of a soul functioning inside a
living human being, and argued that we
cannot step into the same river twice.
Xenophanes of Colophon famously claimed
that:

If oxen and horses or lions had hands, and could paint with their hands, and produce works of art as men do, horses would paint the forms of gods like horses, and oxen like oxen...

Unfortunately the writings of these earlier philosophers survive only as fragments. Socrates benefits from his student, Plato, whose vivid portrayals of Socrates in his dialogues preserve the thoughts and personality of the philosopher who wrote nothing down himself. Socrates was not merely a philosopher. In a society where political power was based on personality and the strength of one's arguments, Socrates was a danger to political and social stability. Aristophanes portrayed him in his Clouds as one who showed how someone could 'make the weaker argument stronger'. Socrates was associated with Pericles and after Pericles' death he progressively fell from favour. It didn't help that many of those associated with

Socrates later became opponents of Athenian democracy. In the end Socrates was brought to trial, accused of introducing new gods and corrupting young men, and sentenced to death. He was forced to drink hemlock.

Plato (429–347 BC) was more than just Socrates's mouthpiece. Plato's large body of work uses Socrates as a character to advance ideas – how far they are Socrates's and how far Plato's will never be known. Plato wrote on politics, on ethics, on epistemology and on religion – among many other subjects. His ideas are still relevant to political and philosophical debate today, and with Socrates and Aristotle, he is part of the foundation of the western intellectual tradition.

The third great philosopher, Aristotle (384–322 BC), was born in Chalcidice. He travelled to Athens as a teenager to join Plato's Academy, a school where the great thinker taught his students. Aristotle, more than any other philosopher, was influential on western intellectual development. His great body of writing covers virtually all endeavours known to man at that point in history. He writes on anything and everything from poetry to science, politics to zoology. Apart from his writing, Aristotle was famous as a teacher. His Macedonian birthplace and fame as a great thinker led Philip II of Macedon to employ him as tutor to his son, the future Alexander the Great.

In the field of history Athens played as great a role. The historian Herodotus is thought to have spent time in Athens during the early years of the Peloponnesian War (circa 430 BC). An early combatant of that war was Thucydides who rose to become one of the ten Athenian generals for the year 424 BC and, as a result of his failure to save the town of Amphipolis from the Spartan commander Brasidas, was exiled. During this exile he began to write his History of the Peloponnesian War 'in the belief that it was going to be a great war and more worth writing about than any of those which had taken place in the past.' Thucydides was correct in his opinion although a part of the reason for its greatness is because it has a truly great historian to chronicle it. He died before the end of it. The third notable Greek historian was another Athenian, Xenophon – and, like Thucydides he too had some direct experience of war. Xenophon attempted to complete Thucydides' history (in his own Hellenica) not long after the latter's death but it is for his adventurous autobiographical history of an army of Greek mercenaries trying to fight their way home from the heart of Persian territory, the Anabasis, that he is chiefly remembered.

Athens was thus the cultural centre of the world. Among its inhabitants were some of the greatest thinkers, writers and artists. The most beautiful buildings and sculptures filled its streets. It was the richest of city-states, the most powerful among the Greeks, the leader of a confederation that had defeated the great Persian army. And politically it was the most advanced democracy of its day. Sparta was to dissolve this dream of an ideal society, with a little help from the Athenians' own arrogance.

The Classical World: Sparta

Sparta's celebrations after the defeat of the Persians were short-lived. Its role as co-leader with Athens against the Persian menace was damaged by the behaviour of two of its leaders, Pausanias and Leotychidas. Leotychidas led a force against Persian allies soon after the Persian War but he was quickly recalled to face allegations of bribery. Pausanias took part in the battle at Plataea and displeased his fellow Spartans with his overestimation of his own role in that conflict. The next year (478 BC) he was sent in charge of a Greek fleet against the Persians at Byzantium. He was accused of treachery through plotting with the Persian enemy and the other Greeks with him mutinied in response to his acts. Sparta called him back home where he was tried and found innocent of any wrongdoing. Back in Byzantium, representing the Spartans, the Athenian leader Cimon expelled Pausanias after more evidence of his scheming with the enemy came to light. Pausanias retired to Ionia rather than Sparta this time. Soon more accusations of collaboration (and the claim that he was now wearing Persian dress) followed. Back he went to Sparta, where he was again found innocent. Sparta's reputation was in tatters over its inability to deal with him effectively. Eventually he was convicted of plotting a revolt with the helots, to whom he promised full citizenship, and sentenced to death.

Sparta's problems with the helots were unsurprising, and went back centuries. Sparta's expansion in the ninth and eighth centuries as it strove to make Laconia, the south-eastern corner of the Peloponnese, a Spartan homeland was aggressive. Initially conquered towns were required to provide soldiers for the Spartan cause but essentially retained their freedoms. With the capture of the town of Helos the Spartans altered their attitude to the losers. From now on, the inhabitants of defeated towns were made slaves of Sparta – 'helots'. This policy continued when the Spartan moved west to take the region of Messenia.

In some respects the helots were in a worse position than slaves. Individual Spartans controlled particular helots but, as each helot was a slave of the state, they could not be freed, as was the case in other Greek states. Religion and law prevented the Spartans from dealing with the helots as they saw fit. To get around this problem the ephors officially declared war on the helots once a year, to enable any helot's punishment or execution without guilt falling on the Spartan who did the deed. In addition, there was a Spartan equivalent of the secret police, the krypteia, who sought out and executed helots thought to be a threat to the public order.

The constant fear of a helot rebellion

prevented Sparta from taking a greater role abroad like Athens. While many city-states were busy setting up colonies in the eighth century, the only Spartan colony originating from that time was at Taras, a colony formed by Sparta as somewhere to send the rebellious Partheniai.

Apart from the helots, Sparta's relations with its neighbours were often poor. By 470 BC Peloponnesian solidarity in the face of Persian aggression had vanished when the state of Elis, most of the state of Arcadia, and the city of Argos allied themselves against the Spartans. No sooner had the Spartans defeated the Arcadians than a great earthquake struck at the Spartan homeland whereupon the Messenian helots chose to mount a substantial rebellion. It took Sparta's allies, the might of Athens, and a five-year campaign to restore order. Spartan military prowess was much admired but the Spartans were not much loved.

The Spartan army was equipped and

organised much as other Greek armies were: the infantry equipped with spears and shields, greaves for the legs, plumed helmets and breastplates for protection. These soldiers were called hoplites, and the group in battle they were organised into was called a phalanx. There were also peltasts (equipped with a lighter shield, the pelte, and javelins which were thrown at the enemy) and sling-throwers. What made the difference was that in a city-state like Athens, military service was generally a brief, two-year interlude before joining the citizenry. In Sparta it was much more.

In Sparta a child could expect to be taken from its parents at the age of seven and put through the agoge, the public upbringing. From the age of 7 to 17 they were paides, receiving an essentially military training that was leavened somewhat by teaching in music and dance. At the age of 12 they entered into a relationship with an older adult male. (Homosexuality was accepted throughout the

Greek world – Sparta and Thebes institution-alised it within their army structure.) From 18 to 19 they were paidiskoi, eligible to fight as reservists or join the krypteia. From 20 to 29 they were hebontes, full members of the army, and although they could marry, had to live with their fellow soldiers in messes refered to as sysskania. The situation with the helots reinforced this system. The Spartans needed the helots to work the land to support a society where every male under 30 was a soldier; the Spartans needed such a military society to keep control of the helots. This rigorous upbringing was unparalleled in Greece – the closest experience was to be had in Thebes. The Spartans were the hardmen of Ancient Greece. The arts had withered there in comparison to the explo-sion in Athens. They lacked colonies, they lacked Athens' wealth. But their military prowess was respected, and even their defeats, like Thermopylae, added to their lustre.

While the Athenians enjoyed the benefits of the Delian League, the Spartans had negotiated many alliances, often with fellow Dorian states, to such an extent that they could be said to have had a league of their own, the Peloponnesian League (although the term is a modern invention – at the time references are made to the 'Spartans and their allies'). And so by the time of the Peloponnesian War, virtually all of Greece was committed to either one faction or the other.

The Peloponnesian War

The Peloponnesian War proper commenced in 431 BC. Conflict had broken out before this, however. In 461 BC Athens had fought with Corinth over the latter's aggression towards the town of Megara. Sparta, as Corinthian allies, had been pulled into the fight. The Thirty Years Peace, agreed between Athens and Sparta in 445 BC, finally ended this war. Nothing was really resolved by the treaty agreed then, as became clear later on.

Athens and Corinth fell out again in 433 BC over Athenian attempts to extort money from Corinthian colonies. Athens broke some of the pledges it had made as part of the Peace and consequently Sparta threatened war. The Athenians, wealthy, confident, with the greatest Greek navy and a heavily refortified city, were unwilling to back down. Pericles banged the drum convincingly in the cause of Athenian nationalism. Greece paused on the edge of civil war. Then Thebes, a Spartan ally, made a move on the small town of Plataea, an ally of Athens. It was the start of the war.

The Peloponnesian War ran from 431–404 BC. The first ten years, a phase referred to as the Archidamian War after one of the Spartan kings involved, Archidamus II, began with frequent invasions of Attica by the Spartan army. The Athenians, wary of direct confrontation, chose to retreat behind their walls in response. Once the Spartans had laid waste to the countryside there was nothing for them to do but go home. Unfortunately nature undid the Athenian plan. The great number of people (estimated at 300,000) crowded together in the city made a breeding ground for disease. In 430 BC the plague broke out. As Thucydides described:

'They died like flies. The bodies of the dying were heaped one on top of the other, and half-dead creatures could be seen staggering about in the streets or flocking around the fountains in their desire for water. The temples... were full of the dead bodies of people who had died inside them... Many people, lacking the necessary means of burial because so many deaths had occurred in their households, adopted the most shameless methods. They would arrive first at a funeral pyre that had been made by others, put their own dead upon it and set it alight...'

Pericles died from this plague in 429 BC. After a brief recovery, the plague then came back in 427 BC and killed even more people. Pericles' death left a vacuum at the heart of Athenian politics. It was filled by the infamous demagogue, Cleon, who showed what stuff he was made of in 427 BC. In that year a failed rebellion occurred at Mytilene on Lesbos, aimed at replacing the pro-Athenian leadership. The Athenians during assembly debated as to how they could show their displeasure at this wavering of support in an ally. Cleon argued that the most suitable response was to execute all of the adult males in the city and enslave the women and children. The assembly agreed, and sent a force to execute the punishment. This force had landed at Lesbos and was making preparations when a messenger suddenly arrived with instructions to ignore the order – the Athenians had come to their senses in the end. Cleon made a very effective career out of appealing to the crowd's worst instincts.

Despite the plague, the Athenian policy of attempting to avoid direct conflict except through their navy (which effectively harried Spartan shipping and coastal settlements) was paying off. Sparta managed to conquer Plataea but achieved little else. Athens upped the ante – they took the war to Sicily, attacking Syracuse, and continued with their efforts in the Peloponnese. Sparta was on the verge of suing for peace when their new leader, Brasidas, succeeded in winning victories in Chalcidice to the north in 424 BC. Some reluctant Athenian allies, heartened by the Spartan success, took the opportunity to revolt. An Athenian force was sent out under Cleon to win back the town of Amphipolis. In the ensuing battle, both Cleon and Brasidas were killed. Back in Athens, the most influential politician left now that Cleon was dead was Nicias, a moderate. He took advantage of the death of the most aggressive figures on each side to negotiate a peace that was named after him, the Peace of Nicias, in 421 BC. It was supposed to last 50 years but within two years, small conflicts had broken out between the two sides. By 415 BC a great Athenian army had landed on Sicily. The war had recommenced.

Back in Athens, a new figure had risen in the public arena to challenge Nicias. This was the brilliant Alcibiades, a renowned warrior, associated with Pericles, as handsome as he was clever, and as brave as he was unscrupulous. After agitating throughout the brief period of peace, he was the main force behind the attack launched on Sicily and was sent out as one of the generals to take command. Before he left, an act of sacrilege took place one night in Athens. Roadside statues of the god Hermes (patron of travellers) were mutilated. Alcibiades' enemies sought to put him in the frame for this desecration. They finally managed to have him recalled from Sicily, not long after he arrived there. On the way back he slipped his captors. In his absence he was found guilty of the act and sentenced to death. Alcibiades had little choice but to join the other side.

With the Spartans he proved as effective a military leader as he had done with the Athenians. He wisely suggested they support Syracuse in Sicily as the Athenian force, ironically led by Nicias (who had opposed the expedition), threatened to overwhelm it. A remarkable change in fortune led to the Syracusans with their allies delivering a devastating blow when they destroyed the Athenian fleet off Syracuse. One of the most poignant parts of the History of the Peloponnesian War is where Thucydides describes the plight of the Athenian army on land, having witnessed the destruction of the vessels they hoped would take them home. They are forced to flee inland, leaving their dead and wounded comrades behind on the beach, yet knowing that they are only fleeing deeper into enemy territory, and that an inevitable defeat and destruction awaits them there. In the end their only options were death or slavery. This was a major catastrophe for the Athenians, yet still they continued the war.

Alcibiades had soon alienated his hosts (seducing the wife of one of the two Spartan kings did not help) and moved east. In Sardis he was trying to undermine the Athenian democracy by plotting to get Persian support in helping to finance a revolution by officers of the fleet. The revolution did take place in 411 BC and control of Athens passed to an oligarchy called the Four Hundred after numerous prominent democrats were murdered. The Four Hundred were overthrown by the Five Thousand and they in turn were replaced by the restoration of democracy in 410 BC. Alcibiades had been abandoned early on by the oligarchs, and hence survived their fall – helped by his involvement in two Athenian naval victories over the Spartans at Abydos (411 BC) and Cyzicus (410 BC). In 407 BC he returned to Athens to receive a huge welcome and the overall command of the Athenian war machine. Two years later his advice before the Battle of Aegospotami was ignored, the Athenians lost to the Spartan admiral Lysander (the Athenians lost 160 of 180 ships – 4,000 of their men were captured and put to death), and effectively the war was over. Lysander moved on Athens. The Athenians were besieged on land and sea. The corn supply had been cut off and famine threatened. Their allies had deserted them. They finally surrendered in April 404 BC. Alcibiades had fled for safety to the court of a Persian governor in Asia Minor – and was eventually murdered there, some say at the Spartans' behest.

The Spartans resisted calls for the destruction of Athens. Instead they placed another oligarchy in power, the Thirty Tyrants. The democracy was restored before too long but in their brief period in charge the Thirty had executed some 1,500 political opponents. The new democracy took its revenge by executing friends and associates of the oligarchs. One of them was Socrates.

The Late Classical Age

The age of Athens as a great political force was over. Culturally it still shone but political leadership had passed to Sparta. The Spartans, at the instigation of their King, Agesilaos II, soon turned their attention to new enemies. One of the first of these was Persia where they tried to influence the succession by supporting the younger son of the late Emperor Darius against the newly-crowned Artaxerxes II. As is recounted in Xenophon's Anabasis, 10,000 Greek mercenaries followed Cyrus up country to finally confront the enemy not far from Babylon. Cyrus lost and was killed, and the Greeks then faced a long journey back through hostile territory. The scene where they finally reach the sea and thus freedom is one of the most famous in Greek literature.

Sparta's failure in Persia did not dissuade them from trying to exert influence elsewhere. In Greece, in Sicily where they supported the tyrant Dionysios I of Syracuse, and probably in Egypt too, they tried to mimic the behaviour of Athens years before. Soon they had their own enemies at home. The Corinthian War started in 395 BC. Corinth was not pleased by Sparta's interference in its Syracusan colony, and managed to get support from Argos, Boeotia, Athens and Persia. Artaxerxes was instrumental in negotiating the end of this war in 386 BC (hence its description as the King's Peace) when, in essence, Sparta agreed to keep out of Persian affairs and vice versa.

Gradually antipathy built up between Sparta and Thebes. Sparta had supported a coup at Thebes. Shortly after those Thebans removed from power – with aid from Athens – took the city back. Sparta tried to exact its revenge on a number of occasions but the united front presented by Athens and Thebes held them off. Athens, anxious at the Spartan threat, tried to resurrect another Delian League in miniature: the Second Athenian

League. It proved unnecessary. Thebes' reputation as a military force was growing. They
had created an elite fighting force, the Sacred
Band, comprised of 150 pairs of male lovers,
supported by the state (the theory was that by
having the lovers fight side by side they would
fight all the harder). The crucial battle was at
Leuctra in 371 BC where, under their leader
Epaminondas and with the use of cavalry and
the Sacred Band, the Thebans comprehen-
sively defeated the Spartans. The myth of
Spartan invincibility on the battlefield was
over.

Thebes' period as supreme Greek power
was short. In ten years with Epaminondas
leading an army in the Peloponnese to the
south, and Pelopidas fighting in the north
against both Thessaly and Macedonia, they
won battle after battle. Most notably
Messenia was freed from the Spartan yoke in
369 BC. Within a two-year period both of
these inspirational leaders were killed in
battle and with them went Theban

supremacy. For a brief time Caria in Asia Minor became the centre of attention under its cunning and wealthy leader Mausolus. Athens futilely tried to step into Thebes' empty shoes. Mausolus's plotting induced a number of islands, members of the Second Athenian League, to revolt. Athens sent a fleet under its general Chares, and the brief Social War (357–355 BC) began. After the Athenian defeat at Embata in 356 BC, the Persians threatened to step in. The Athenians, unable to even contemplate a war with Persia, surrendered, and then returned to Athens humiliated.

The old powers of Greece were spent as major forces. The new leaders of Greece were to come from the north, Macedonia, and were considered by their sophisticated relations to the south to be little more than rustic cousins. One man was to mastermind their ascendancy in Greece – Philip II.

From the start of his reign (359 BC) Philip was put to the test. In his first year he had to defeat a combined force of mercenaries and Athenians who were attempting to put a pretender on the Macedonian throne. With Athens occupied with the Social War, Philip turned his attention to his immediate east in Chalcidice, capturing first the city of Amphipolis, then Poteidaia, then Methone (354 BC). He gained control of the gold mines there, an important source of funds. At this time conflict had blown up in the south between Thebes and Phocis. Thebes had used the excuse of Phocis's 'cultivation of sacred land' to try and ensure that the Delphic Amphictiony (a league of city-states who ensured the proper maintenance of and behaviour towards the sanctuary at Delphi) would fine Phocis. The fine was more than Phocis could pay. Thebes greedily grasped the opportunity of leading a 'Sacred War' against Phocis as punishment and then were wrong-footed when Phocis raided the temple treasury at Delphi and used the sizeable funds to hire a mercenary force large enough to repel the Thebans. After Phocis sought to further bolster its position with a treaty with the Thessalian city of Pherae, another city of Thessaly, Larissa, sought to safeguard its position in turn by calling in support from Macedonia.

Philip came down with his army. After one unexpected defeat he quickly availed himself of the opportunity to conquer all of Thessaly, adding its military resources to his own. Only a force of Athenians at the narrow pass of Thermopylae held him back (352 BC). He returned north and continued his campaigns there. By 346 BC Philip was back at Thermopylae, having tied the Athenians up with peace negotiations. The gains continued: while making further conquests in the north he promoted rebellion in the south, supporting Messenia and Megalopolis against Sparta and a rebel faction in Elis, among others. Thrace fell to him. By 340 BC he was attacking Byzantium which threatened the Athenian supply of grain from the regions around the Black Sea. Finally Athens and Thebes agreed to confront him. Philip marched back to central Greece where a part of his army met the Greek forces at Chaeronea. Athens was beaten, Thebes crushed. Philip was now the effective ruler of Greece. He called a conference at Corinth and formed a League of Corinth comprised of the beaten Greek states that, unsurprisingly, elected him leader. They had little other choice in the matter. He stationed troops in various locales throughout central Greece to guarantee the peace. And at the conference he announced his plan to conquer Persia. This final ambition was to prove beyond him. Philip had fallen out with both his wife, Olympias, and his young son and heir, Alexander: either or both of them could have been behind his subsequent assassination.

Greece rejoiced at the news of his death, sensing freedom ahead.

Alexander the Great

On becoming King, Alexander was forced to prove his mettle much as his father had years before. His eyes were on Persia but first he struck out against the nearby Illyrians. Rumours that he had been killed in this first campaign began to travel south. Thebes, still resentful at the brevity of its period of supreme glory, thought to take advantage of this 'death' by rising up against Macedonian oppression. Alexander was on the scene in no time with his army and made Thebes an example that none of the other Greeks were likely to forget for a while. He destroyed the city and enslaved its inhabitants. Leaving now for the east, he felt confident leaving his empire in the hands of his father's faithful lieutenant, Antipater.

In 334 BC, with an army of some 40,000 infantry and 5,000 cavalry, he crossed over the Hellespont into Asia Minor. Alexander was always aware of the importance of the symbolic – once in Asia he claimed it by thrusting his spear into the soil. He visited what were claimed to be the tombs of Ajax and Achilles at Troy, behaving as if his own expeditionary force was a later version of Agamemnon's.

The first battle was with a large force lead by various satraps (provincial governors) of the Persian emperor. They awaited Alexander's army on the banks of the river Granicus. They were easily defeated. Alexander led the right wing of his army personally, inspiring his men by his own heroic example. But the deciding factor was probably Alexander's secret weapon, passed on from his father. Philip had caused his men to abandon the usual Greek spear and instead adopt the sarisa, twice the size, a six-metre long pike. Organised into tight phalanxes, the front row of men thus had four rows of these vicious weapons before them. As long as the infantry's discipline held, they were virtually unbeatable.

Little opposition faced him in the after-math of this battle. His army proceeded to wind its way through Asia Minor, only receiving more than token resistance at the coastal city of Halicarnassus, where the Persian fleet managed to keep the defenders well supplied and supported. At Gordion the most notable event was the story of Alexander's solving of the riddle of the Gordian Knot. A prophecy held that whoever untangled this intricate knot on an old chariot would rule Asia. Alexander is supposed to have fulfilled the prophecy by using his sword to cut through it.

Darius, Persia's ruler, finally confronted Alexander with his army at the southeastern border of Asia Minor – at Issus. The superior numbers of the Persians became a disadvantage when they were lured by Alexander into the narrow plain there. Darius and his army fled. Alexander was content to let them go for now. He continued south along the Levantine coast. Alexander's policy towards opposition was fairly straightforward: fight rather than negotiate. He made examples of each city that resisted him, and this began to have an effect. By the time he reached Egypt there was little opposition. He founded a new city there, Alexandria, on the coast (he was to found literally dozens of new cities named after himself in this way). Here again he helped in the creation of his own legend. Alexander headed out into the western desert with a few companions to the oracle at the oasis at Siwa where he was declared to be the son of the Egyptian god Amun.

With Egypt made his own, it was time to head back east and finally deal with Darius. He invaded Mesopotamia and caught the Persian army at Gaugamela (331 BC). Again they were routed, again Darius fled, and again Alexander chose not to pursue. He headed deeper into Mesopotamia, taking Babylon and then Susa until he finally marched into Persepolis, the capital, capturing the vast treasury of the Persians. He stayed there for five months, enjoying the sophisticated pleasures of Persian life and watching Darius's great palace burn. Darius was soon dead. He fled to the edge of the empire that was once his, where one of his satraps, Bessus of Bactria, murdered him and delivered the body up to the Greeks.

Alexander had exacted revenge for Persia's invasions of Greece in the early fifth century. This would have had some political significance at home where a lonely attempt at revolution in his absence by the Spartans had been effectively and brutally put down by Antipater.

The size of the conquered territories of the east, and the speed with which Alexander progressed ever onwards made it difficult to institute major organisational changes in these newly conquered provinces. Alexander kept to the satrapy system, generally appointing Greek rulers (although on occasions he preferred a native, or even sometimes allowed the existing satrap to rule) supported by a small body of Macedonians.

To the east and north rebellion stirred. Bessus claimed the succession to Darius and another satrap, Satibarzanes, attempted to revolt. Alexander had adopted Persian dress and some of their manners, a fact that went down badly with some of the Macedonian nobility who had accompanied him (at least one conspiracy had to be put down with executions). Dealing with both Alexander pushed northwards into distant territory north of the Hindu Kush. There he founded Alexandriaescharta, 'Alexandria the Farthest', and as was the case elsewhere, encouraged Greeks to settle in this land thousands of miles away from home, intending this policy of colonisation to secure his control of such a huge empire. More revolts occurred and the strain began to tell. The Greeks had crossed into Asia six years ago and were understandably homesick. Alexander's drinking became notorious – in one drunken argument he killed one of his oldest friends,

Cleitus, whom he had recently appointed
Bessus's successor as satrap of Bactria. To the
Persians Alexander was a god but the Greeks
found his playing up to that role sacrilegious.
Ever onward they went, this time east,
towards India.

In 326 BC Alexander's men reached the
Indus valley on the edge of the Punjab. At the
Battle of the Hydaspes he defeated the Indian
King Porus, meeting elephants in battle for
the first time. They pushed on as far as the
Hyphasis River. By now Alexander was the
only one wanting to go on. The army was
near mutinous. He finally agreed to go back,
choosing a southern route through the
Gedrosian Desert. The fleet, under
Alexander's admiral Nearchus, sailed back
from the mouth of the Indus, across the
Arabian Sea and up the length of the Persian
Gulf. Nearchus was lucky: the march back
led through some of the most inhospitable
territory on earth, for which the
Macedonians were ill-equipped. Many died.

They arrived back in Persepolis in 324 BC. Alexander started building up a fleet in the Levant. Some of these ships were brought to Babylon in 323 BC and it is likely that Alexander intended to use these to expand into Arabia. It was rumoured that the rest of the fleet intended to sail west, aiming to conquer Southern Italy and Carthage. Alexander's sudden death that year put a stop to this. He was 32 years old. Some put it down to poison but the common view was that he had simply drunk himself to death. He'd conquered an Empire the like of which the world had never seen before. He left a newborn son as heir, ensuring a fight over the succession. In the later years of his campaign Alexander had discarded much of his Greek identity, and so had his army. Many of the most senior positions were held by Macedonians but the army itself was comprised of a mixture of peoples. Many of the Macedonians and Greeks had chosen Persian wives, had stopped and settled down and were raising families in the east. Alexander's lasting legacy was this hybrid empire, Greek and Persian, that – more than anything – was to embody the period that followed his death.

The Hellenistic Age and Afterwards

4. The Hellenistic Age and Afterwards

The Early Hellenistic World

Hellenism can best be described as the fusion of Greek with non-Greek – an accurate description of the world Alexander left. Immediately after Alexander's death his son was declared King Alexander IV to reign jointly with his uncle (Alexander the Great's half-brother), Philip III Arrhidaeus. Unfortunately the former had yet to enjoy his first birthday while the latter was mentally-impaired. Antipater, though he had fallen out with Alexander before his death, was the power behind the throne in Greece. In Persia, Alexander's generals eyed each other nervously. The first to take advantage was Ptolemy who, guessing that the empire would fall apart sooner or later, managed to obtain the position of Governor of Egypt. His plan was that when the Empire did split he would be in a good position to establish an independent kingdom there. In Babylon power was shared between Craterus and Perdiccas, with the latter the official regent. Antigonus Monophthalmos ('one-eyed') was still in charge of Phrygia (Asia Minor). Lysimachus was made governor of Thrace. Two other leading figures, Seleucus and Leonnatus, bided their time. Soon the game of succession started for real – the object was to be among the last survivors.

First Greek settlers in Bactria tried to revolt, wanting to return home. This rebellion was put down. Then Athens led a rebellion of states against Macedonia which developed into the Lamian War (323– 322BC). Before Antipater could put this revolution down, Leonnatus leapt in ostensibly to help out with the suppression but probably with more selfish intent at heart. He was killed in battle. Antipater won and crushed the rebellion, from then on keeping an even tighter control on the Greeks. (Demosthenes, the great Athenian orator, who had spent most of his adult life pushing the cause of independence finally committed suicide at this political setback.) Craterus was killed in battle. Perdiccas assassinated. Antipater took over as regent; Antigonus took overall control of the army. Seleucus had, by this point, managed to obtain the position of governor of Babylon. Antipater died in 319 BC: his successor, Polyperchon, managed to make a political mess when he tried to win Greek loyalty by loosening the Macedonian reins. The Athenians celebrated their new freedoms by using them to execute those among them who were pro-Macedonian. Eumenes, Alexander's rich ex-secretary, allied himself with Polyperchon and together they took on Antigonus. They managed to capture Babylon, sending Seleucus running to Egypt before Eumenes himself was killed and Polyperchon supplanted by Cassander, Antipater's son. Cassander had Alexander the Great's mother, Olympias, executed (she had already engineered the murder of her stepson, Philip III Arrhidaeus) and Alexander IV and his mother Roxane kept under guard.

Antigonus was now viewed by the others to have become too powerful. Lysimachus, Cassander and Ptolemy made an alliance and together spent four years fighting him (315–311 BC). Neither side could finish off the other. Seleucus won back Babylon but was then pushed out of the picture when the four leaders arranged a peace. Ptolemy got Egypt and Cyprus; Lysimachus, Thrace; Antigonus, Asia; and Cassander, Macedon and Greece until Alexander IV reached maturity.

Cassander then proceeded to have Alexander and his mother killed in around 308BC but succesfully kept the news of the death of the King quiet for two years. He also put the Aristotelian philosopher, Demetrius of Phaleron, in charge of Athens. To the east, Seleucus was losing territory to the Indian King Chandragupta Maurya. Antigonus persisted as a thorn in the others' sides and he now had an ally who was a military genius, his son Demetrius Poliorcetes ('the Besieger').

In 301 BC, a concerted effort by Cassander, Seleucus, Ptolemy and Lysimachus (with the help of Indian war-elephants) finally defeated and killed Antigonus and sent his son fleeing to the Levant where he managed to successfully keep the four and their forces at bay. They all declared themselves kings now, following Antigonus's self-declaration some years before. The four now proceeded to divide up Antigonus's territory amongst themselves.

Cassander's death in 297 BC gave the Besieger an opportunity to make a move on Greece, most of which he'd conquered before being repelled. He tried the same approach in Asia and again nearly accomplished his aims before ill-health compelled him to give up and surrender to Seleucus (who encouraged him to drink himself to death). Seleucus and Lysimachus fell out with each other and the latter was subsequently killed in battle. This conflict was partly the result of scheming by a grandson of Ptolemy's, Ptolemy Ceraunus (the Thunderbolt), who after Lysimachus's death managed both to convince Lysimachus's army to support him and to assassinate Seleucus.

In the early 270s, a force from outside was to provide a certain sense of unity. Migrating Celtic tribes were beginning to make their way down into Greece – some actually getting into Asia Minor. A treaty between Antigonus Gonatus, the most powerful man in Greece and the son of Demetrius Poliorcetes, and Antiochus I, son of Seleucus, led to a common and successful war against the invaders (although they were unable to prevent a certain degree of colonisation by the Celts in Thrace among other areas).

Finally a state of stability began to prevail,

based around the three powers: the Antigonids in Macedonia, the Seleucids in Syria and the Ptolemies in Egypt.

Ptolemaic Egypt

Egypt's natural resources made it the richest of the three successor (a term used to refer to those who succeeded Alexander) kingdoms with a thriving, mercantile economy. It was also the last of the Hellenic kingdoms to fall under the control of the Romans. The early Ptolemies were notable patrons of the arts and sciences and at Alexandria they founded a great library that was to be the centre of Greek scholarship throughout the Hellenic world. Although Greeks initially held all the senior roles – and it was to be some while before a Ptolemaic ruler could even speak the native language – Egyptians were increasingly able to rise to positions of prominence although it is also true to say that the Egyptians in these positions were increasingly

Hellenised. Greek was the language of the bureaucracy, and an Egyptian could not get on without a command of it. Occasionally Egyptian nationalism raised its head. For twenty years at the end of the third century Upper Egypt enjoyed native rule, supported by the kingdom of Meroe to the south, until Ptolemy V reconquered the territory.

In its last century of independence, feuding among the royals became an equal opportunity endeavour. The famous Cleopatria (Cleopatria VII) was not the first female royal to be as formidable as the males in the family. She was the last Ptolemaic ruler, and not the first to have to use Rome to bolster her rule. Cunning as Cleopatria was, Rome overcame her. Julius Caesar she bent to her will; after his assassination, her involvement with his fellow Roman Mark Antony was to prove fatal. Rome had accepted Egypt as an ally but, when Cleopatria and Antony appeared to be conspiring to make Egypt the ruler of an Eastern Empire, Octavian and his fleet were sent to deal with them. The naval battle between the two sides at Actium (31 BC) was to see Octavian (later to be known as the Emperor Augustus) and Rome triumphant. Egypt became a Roman province from that date, marking the end of the Hellenistic Age.

The Library at Alexandria

Alexandria became famous as the greatest of the Greek cities. It lay on a strip of land between Lake Mareotis and the Mediterranean Sea. It was divided into five parts, each name after one of the first five letters of the Greek alphabet (Alpha, Beta, Gamma, Delta and Epsilon). Beta was the most prestigious area as it contained the Palace. In addition Alexandria had a stadium, a theatre, a racecourse, the tomb of Alexander and a zoo – but it was the Library that was prized above all in the Ancient World.

The Library was part of the Alexandrian

Museum, an institute where state-supported scholars engaged in literary research. The Library proper is estimated to have contained something in the region of 500,000 rolled-up scrolls (the equivalent of somewhere in the region of 100,000 books). Competition between libraries, especially between Alexandria and its nearest competitor at Pergamum, was fierce. Ancient authors willed their manuscripts to Alexandria, thinking it the securest guarantee of their work's safety. Besides the librarian, a team of assistants, slaves, restorers and copyists worked there. Visitors were allowed to consult but not remove books and the libraries generally kept regular opening hours. Scholars at Alexandria tried to establish a canon of Greek poets and poetry, editing the texts, aiming to remove later additions or corruptions. Many of the librarians were poets as well as scholars – Callimachus probably the greatest among them. Callimachus also produced a catalogue of the library's contents: known in later times in Byzantium as the great standard reference work of Greek literature, it is now lost.

Alexandria also had a substantial Jewish population who lived in the Delta quarter. Jewish scholars working with Greeks at the Library were probably responsible for producing the Septuagint, the earliest Greek edition of the Old Testament.

Alexandria was famous for another phenomenal building in addition. At the entrance to its two artificial harbours stood one of the Seven Wonders of the Ancient World, the Pharos of Alexandria.

The Seven Wonders of the World

The Seven Wonders were phenomenal human constructions. The idea dates originally from the Hellenistic World of the second century BC. This celebration of what was primarily Greek greatness was possibly inspired by an earlier list of Greek genius, the Seven Sages.

The Sages were Greeks admired above all others for their wisdom, cleverness or poetic skill. There was often dispute about who should be on the list. While the inclusion of Thales of Miletus, the sixth century scientist, or Solon of Athens, the politician and poet, was uncontroversial, the appearance of Periander the Corinthian tyrant was questioned by more democratically inclined Greeks. Alternate versions of the Seven Sages appeared, with Periander replaced by more politically acceptable individuals. These replacements were, in turn, questioned. One, Myson of Chen, was criticised as possessing only one outstanding quality – he was 'famous for his obscurity.'

The Pharos – a great lighthouse – appeared on later lists of the Seven Wonders. The other wonders were: the Pyramids at Giza; the Hanging Gardens of Babylon; Phidias's statue of Zeus at Olympia; Mausolus's tomb, the Mausoleum of Halicarnassus; the Temple of Artemis at Ephesus; and the Colossus of Rhodes. Only the Pyramids now remain.

The Seleucid Kingdom

Little change occurred in the organisation of the Seleucid Kingdom until the reign of Antiochus III (223–187 BC). Antiochus instituted reforms to what was essentially the old Persian bureaucracy. The satraps were replaced by strategoi, generals, combining military and political functions. Two cities became administrative centres: Sardis in the west and Seleucia in the east. Greek culture became increasingly important, overriding local identity to a great extent. Antiochus IV put up a statue to Zeus in the temple at Jerusalem: the revolt that happened as a result of this act led over two decades later to an independent Judea. The problem for its rulers was the size of the Seleucid kingdom – at its greatest extent it linked Greece to India – and the tremendous variety of cultures within it.

Its decline had started early in the third century. First the provinces in the east gained independence – Bactria, Sogdia and Parthia.

In the west Pergamon gained independence, as did Cappadocia and Pontos. More and more of Asia Minor was lost. In the east Parthia grew, swallowing up more and more of Seleucia. Rome's presence began to be felt. As the Roman Empire grew it moved further eastwards. Antiochus III briefly recaptured some of the independent territory lost in Asia Minor and then was beaten in battle again and again by Rome.

Seleucia was barely holding onto Syria and the eastern part of Cilicia when Rome finally conquered it in 64 BC. Antioch, its capital, remained an important city under the Romans. A common culture still existed on both sides on what was now the border between two great empires, Rome and Parthia.

Macedonia

A new force emerged not long after the successor kingdoms had reached a kind of peace in the early third century – Epirus. Epirus's brief moment in the sun was due to the efforts of one of its greatest kings, Pyrrhus. Pyrrhus was great, but not quite great enough. His skills were best deployed internally. He built up a powerful army and state but his actions in the wider world were often a little less than successful. His name became a byword for a too costly victory – a 'pyrrhic' victory.

His successes against the Illyrians and Macedonians brought him to the attention of the Greeks in Southern Italy as a potential saviour in their conflict with Rome. Pyrrhus defeated the Romans at Heraclea and Ausculum with increasingly heavy losses. Syracuse then appealed to him for help in its fight against the Carthaginians, who were at that point allies of Rome. For two years he fought with little to show but the loss of many of his ships before he returned to Southern Italy to continue the fight directly against Rome. Defeated by the Romans this time (at Beneventum) he returned home. Further scheming in Greece was to come to nought. Eventually, while trying to sneak his forces into Argos late one night, the alarm was raised when one of his war-elephants got stuck in the gateway into the city. Pyrrhus's death was less than heroic: an old woman, alarmed at the invasion, hurled a roof tile at his head, killing him. The fate of the elephant is unrecorded.

The third century saw Macedonia and Egypt struggle over control of mainland Greece, with Macedonia the eventual winner. The repulsion of the Celts in 279 BC had involved the growing power of the Aetolians in Greece. Conflict between these Greeks and their stronger opponents, the Macedonians, with their ambitious leader Philip V, led to the former approaching Rome for help in the middle of the First Macedonian War (214–205 BC). A Second Macedonian War (200–196 BC) saw greater Roman involvement, leading afterwards to conflict between the Aetolians and their allies. Rome now encircled the Adriatic Sea, having Illyria as its most easterly province.

The conflict between Rome and Macedonia ended in 168 BC when the Romans finally defeated Philip's son Perseus at Pydna. Southern Greece had looked upon this conflict with little love for either side. The only remaining force in Southern Greece was the Achaean League whose legacy of an alliance with Rome from the days of the Macedonian conflict withered as tensions rose between the two sides. The Achaean War (146–147 BC) saw the destruction of Corinth and the enslavement of its people, the eventual victory of Rome, and the effective end of political independence for Greece.

Rome and Greece

Although Rome won the war, it is debatable as to whether it won the peace. Rome had been exposed to Greek cultural influences since its early days as a result of the colonies in Italy. Conflicts between Rome and Greece saw many Greeks end up as slaves – educated enslaved Greeks were a vehicle for the transmission of Hellenic culture. By the later years of the Roman Republic it was common for Roman senators to be bilingual: often from childhood, taught the language by Greek slaves. Politically and commercially, even after its conquest, the Greek language was the common tongue of the east.

Greek literature had an immeasurable influence on Latin literature. The man seen as the 'father of Roman literature', Lucius Livius Andronicus, was a Greek slave who translated the *Odyssey* into Latin. The major Latin comic poet, Plautus, used the form of the Greek New Comedy for his plays. With Ennius he imported forms of Greek metre to use as models in Roman verse. Early histories written by Roman senators were written in Greek. Even an important religious text like the Sibylline Books was written in Greek. Roman architecture, sculpture, painting, oratory, philosophy (particularly Epicureanism and Stoicism) – virtually every sphere of Roman life was influenced to some extent. Romans even linked their origins back to Trojans who, after the fall of Troy, had been said to have resettled in Latium. The extent to which the influence of Greek was felt can be gauged by the reactions of those like Cato, who urged resistance to the culture of this 'most worthless and unteachable race.' Resistance, at this point, was futile.

Greek literature continued to produce important and influential works itself after the conquest. The novel in Greek is a form that does not arise until the first century AD. Its adherents, writers such as Chariton, Longus and Heliodorus became immensely popular throughout the Roman Empire.

Politically Greece remained within the Empire for centuries. That great lover of Greek culture, the Emperor Nero, gave it its independence back as a mark of his respect in 67 AD – a gift that was reclaimed after Nero's death the following year.

Greece was finally revenged on Rome. In 330 AD the Emperor Constantine I refounded the old Greek city of Byzantium as New Rome, Constantinople. The Roman Empire eventually split into two halves, West and East. In 476 AD the Western Empire fell as Rome was conquered by the Ostrogoths: the Eastern Empire, as much Hellenic and Middle Eastern as it was Roman, was to last nearly another thousand years until it fell to the Turks in 1453.

Recommended Reading
and Further Resources

Recommended Reading
and Further Resources

Primary Texts

Many of the major Ancient Greek authors are published by Penguin or Oxford in paperback translations. A far more extensive selection is kept in print by the Loeb Library in bilingual (Original Greek with English translation on the facing page) hardcover editions – somewhere in the region of 500 volumes. New translations are commissioned all the time, and arguments over which translation displays the greater fidelity are never ending. The best advice is to pick one whose style suits your tastes, and to be aware as to whether the text is abridged or not. Among the essential authors and works are:

Drama

The great Athenian fifth century dramatists –
as has already been mentioned – are the
pinnacle of the Greek dramatic achievement.
Of Aeschylus's seven complete plays the three
forming the Oresteia (Agamemnon, Libation-
Bearers, Eumenides) are essential reading.
Sophocles trilogy of Theban plays detailing the
fall of Oedipus is likewise indispensable. More
of Euripides' plays have survived complete
than those of his two predecessors combined
– one of his most famous is the story of the
tragedy of Medea, the powerful tale of the
revenge of an abandoned woman. Of
Aristophanes' works, the Knights attacks the
demagogue Cleon, Clouds takes on Socrates
while Peace features the famous journey to
heaven on the back of a giant dung beetle
taken by the farmer, Trygaeus. All are recommended. The late fourth century sees the
appearance of Menander, the master of 'New
Comedy' where Aristophanes was the master

of 'Old Comedy'. Until recently with the discovery of his Dyskolos, Menander's plays have only come down to us as fragments – his humour is considerably more suave than Aristophanes'.

History

The finest Greek Historian is Thucydides – his History of the Peloponnesian War is peerless. A fine translation by Rex Warner is published by Penguin: the translation that probably comes closest to the original is that done by Thomas Hobbes. Herodotus tackles the Persian Wars in his History written sometime before Thucydides in the middle of the fifth century. Xenophon continues Thucydides' history in his own Hellenica but his Anabasis is a far more enjoyable read. Of the later historians, Diodorus Siculus's attempt to write a history of the world in the first century is substantial but incomplete and more informative than gripping. Plutarch, an essayist and biographer from Boeotia in the first century AD, wrote a series of Parallel Lives of Greek and Roman heroes which are both an important source of information and an entertaining read. The History of Alexander (the Great) by the second century AD Bithynian Arrian – a Greek historian who served in the Roman army – is another notable later history.

Oratory

The great orator is the Athenian Demosthenes whose surviving fourth century speeches are collected in seven volumes in the Loeb edition. He is an invaluable source on Greek life during that century, let alone the politics of the time. A balance to Demosthenes politically are the writings of Aeschines, who opposed him at the time. Providing similar insights are the speeches of his fellow Athenian, Isocrates, born just before the Peloponnesian War, and the legal specialist Isaeus, born during that same war.

Poetry

Homer's two epic poems – the *Iliad* and *Odyssey* – are essential reading and are available in numerous editions. Two of the more impressive recent translators have been Richmond Lattimore and Robert Fitzgerald and their versions of both poems are highly recommended. A more idiosyncratic but highly enjoyable series of translations of certain books of the *Iliad* have also appeared from the poet Christopher Logue (one such being War Music). From a similar period are the important works of Hesiod, and the anonymous collection of poems called the Homeric Hymns.

A sizeable number of the poems of Pindar (in comparison to many other Greek poets) have survived and represent probably the greatest collection of lyric poetry. Many,

many selections of Ancient Greek poetry are available: Loeb provide a series of anthologies arranged according to form: Greek Bucolic Poets; Greek Elegaic Poetry; Greek Iambic Poetry; and Greek Lyric Poetry. Many of these poems survive as fragments, as is famously the case with the great Ancient Greek woman writer, Sappho.

One extraordinary collection of Greek poetry is the Palatine or Greek Anthology, a collection of thousands of short poems from the time of Homer to the tenth century AD.

Philosophy

The respect in which Plato and Aristotle were held can be measured by the quantity of their work that has come down to us. 12 volumes of Plato are available in Loeb; 23 volumes of Aristotle. Plato is most famous for his political work, the Republic. Other pieces examine a number of different subjects: Theaetetus being concerned with knowledge for instance, the Symposium with love. Aristotle covers an extraordinary range of subjects as the following titles indicate: Metaphysics; Poetics; Physics; On the Heavens; On Colours; Virtues and Vices; Movement of Animals.

The great secondary source of general philosophical knowledge however is the collection of Lives of the Eminent Philosophers by the third century AD Greek philosopher, Diogenes Laertius.

Miscellaneous

In the fields of science the writings of Galen and Hippocrates convey the ancient world's medical ideas, Strabo its geography, while Ptolemy writes of its cosmology. Two volumes of Greek Mathematical Works are published by Loeb, including the writings of such as Euclid, the famed Alexandrian geometrician. One great travel writer belongs to the Roman period, Pausanias, who noted the impressive ruins, art and architecture of Greece in his Description of Greece, the notes from his tour in the middle of the second century AD. Much of the literature of the Roman period tends towards the fantastic: the collection of myths that is the *Library*, mistakenly attributed to Apollodorus of Athens; Apollonius of Rhodes' *Argonautica*, the tale of Jason and his Argonauts; the Hellenistic Romance (examples of which are Longus's *Daphnis and Chloe*, and Chariton's *Callirhoe*); the messianic and magical portrayals of Alexander the Great in the *Alexander Romances*; the fictional letters of Alciphron; the fables of Babrius; the satires of Lucian; the *Dionysiaca of Nonnos*.

Secondary Texts

Boardman, John – Athenian Black Figure Vases (Thames & Hudson)

Boardman, John – Athenian Red Figure Vases: the Archaic Period (Thames & Hudson)

Boardman, John – Athenian Red Figure Vases:

the Classical Period (Thames & Hudson)

Boardman, John, Griffin, Jasper & Murray, Oswyn – The Oxford History of the Classical World (Oxford University Press)

Doumas, Christos The Wall-Paintings of Thera (The Thera Foundation)

Gantz, Timothy – Early Greek Myth (John Hopkins) Vols I & II

Green, Peter – Alexander of Macedon (University of California Press)

Green, Peter – Alexander to Actium – The Hellenistic Age (Thames & Hudson)

Green, Peter – A Concise History of Ancient Greece (Thames & Hudson)

Hornblower, Simon & Spawforth, Antony – The Oxford Classical Dictionary (Oxford University Press)

Morkot, Robert – The Penguin Historical Atlas of Ancient Greece (Penguin)

Papaioannou, Kostas – The Art of Greece (Abrams)

Renfrew, Colin – The Cycladic Spirit (Thames & Hudson)

Taylour, William – The Mycenaeans (Thames & Hudson)

Multimedia and Internet

Perseus 2.0 – Interactive Sources and Studies on Ancient Greece (Yale University Press)

The Oxford Classical Dictionary CD-Rom (Oxford University Press)

Ancient Greece on the Net – http://www.zephryus.demon.co.uk/education/links/hstgr.html

Index

The Athenian Empire

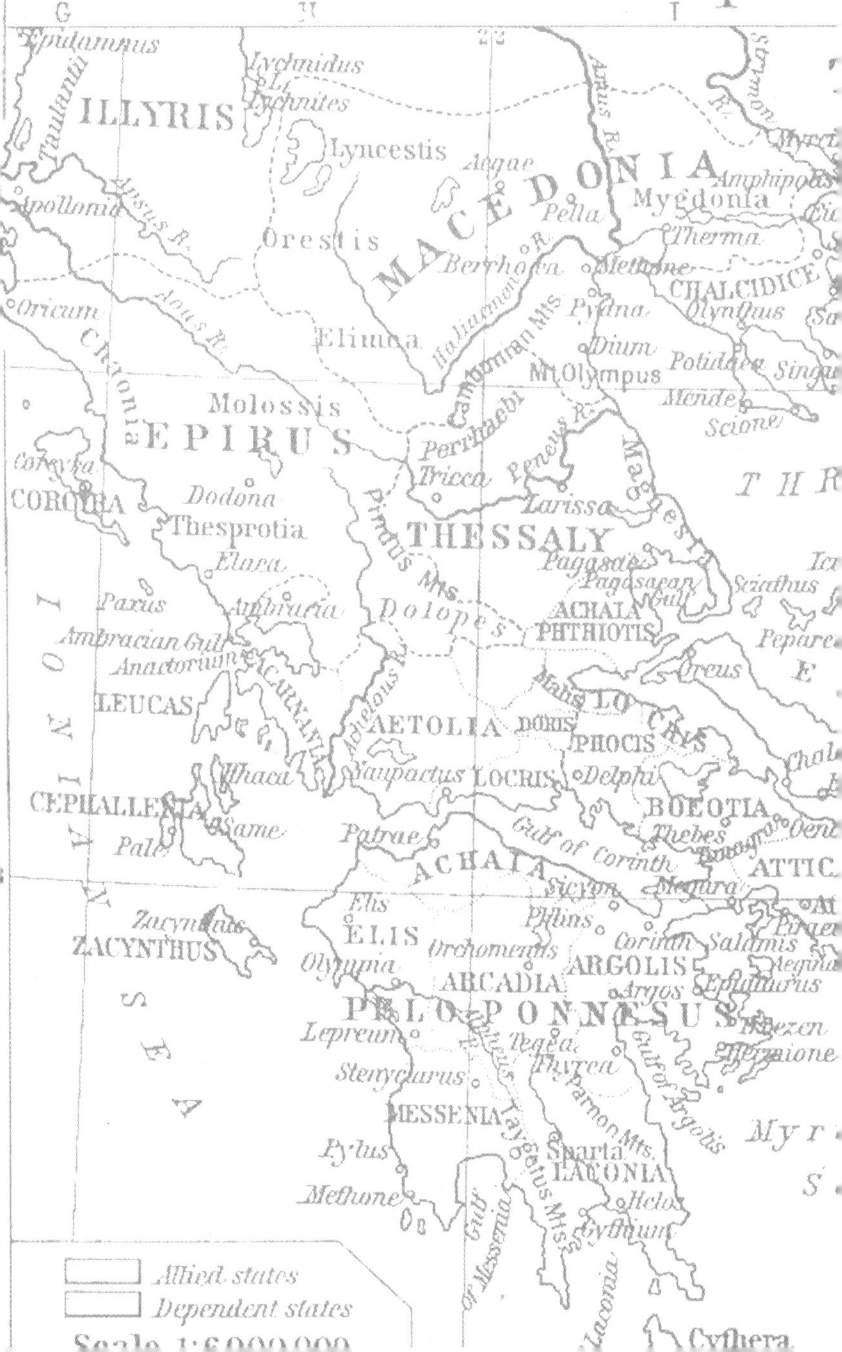